Fodor's InFocus

ARUBA

12
TOP EXPERIENCES

Aruba offers terrific experiences that should be on every traveler's list. Here are Fodor's top picks for a memorable trip.

1 High-Rise Resorts

On a beautiful stretch of Palm Beach, Aruba vacationers can choose among many of the Caribbean's most lavish resorts, with deluxe spas, water-sports centers, fine restaurants, casinos, shops, and nightclubs. (Ch. 5)

2 Eagle Beach

Prepare to be dazzled (seriously, bring your sunglasses) by the bright white sand of Eagle Beach, which stretches far and wide on the south-western coast. The beach is popular but rarely overcrowded. *(Ch. 3)*

3 Casinos

Aruba casinos are the real deal, with slots, table games, and sports books for plenty of action. Theaters, restaurants, bars, and cigar shops round out the entertainment. *(Ch. 7)*

4 Horseback Riding

An exciting, romantic way to explore Aruba is on horseback. Take a leisurely beach ride or survey the countryside on trails flanked by cacti, divi-divi trees, and aloe vera plants. *(Ch. 8)*

5 Barhopping Buses

Why drive to a bar when a groovy bus can pick you up at your hotel? Enjoy the journey and the destination as you're shuttled to the liveliest nightspots aboard Aruba's unique party buses. *(Ch. 6)*

6 The Bonbini Festival

Every week this festival at Fort Zoutman showcases steel pan bands and local performing artists. It's both a brisk introduction to Aruba's lively culture and a great place to meet friendly locals. *(Ch. 6)*

7 Scuba Diving

Advanced and novice divers appreciate the plentiful marine life in Aruba's clear waters. Some of the best sites are right offshore, and there are fascinating shipwrecks in both deep and shallow waters. *(Ch. 8)*

8 Sailing

Day sails to remote snorkeling spots, sunset voyages on a catamaran, and champagne-and-dinner cruises are some of the most memorable ways you can spend a day or night in Aruba. *(Ch. 8)*

9 Dining on the Beach

Open-air dining on the beach is a special island experience available at a number of Aruba restaurants. The most romantic tables are at Passions on the Beach and Flying Fishbone. *(Ch. 4)*

10 Snorkeling

Thanks to water visibility of 90 feet and close-in sites such as Barcadera Reef, snorkelers can view many of the same underwater spectacles as divers. Huge seafans, nurse sharks, and hawksbill turtles are common sights. *(Ch. 8)*

11 Arikok National Park

At Aruba's sprawling national park you can explore caves, play on sand dunes, or hike Mt. Yamanota, the island's highest peak. History you can see includes Arawak petroglyphs and remnants of Dutch settlements. *(Chs. 2, 8)*

12 Oranjestad

Aruba's capital is a delight to explore on foot. Pastel-painted buildings of typical Dutch design face its palm-lined central thoroughfare, and there are numerous boutiques and shops. *(Chs. 2, 9)*

CONTENTS

MAPS

ABOUT THIS GUIDE

Fodor's Recommendations

Everything in this guide is worth doing—we don't cover what isn't—but exceptional sights, hotels, and restaurants are recognized with additional accolades. Fodor'sChoice★ indicates our top recommendations; and **Best Bets** call attention to notable hotels and restaurants in various categories. Care to nominate a new place? Visit Fodors.com/contact-us.

Trip Costs

We list prices wherever possible to help you budget well. Hotel and restaurant price categories from **$** to **$$$$** are noted alongside each recommendation. For hotels, we include the lowest cost of a standard double room in high season. For restaurants, we cite the average price of a main course at dinner or, if dinner isn't served, at lunch. For attractions, we always list adult admission fees; discounts are usually available for children, students, and senior citizens.

Hotels

Our local writers vet every hotel to recommend the best overnights in each price category, from budget to expensive. Unless otherwise specified, you can expect private bath, phone, and TV in your room. For expanded hotel reviews, facilities, and deals visit Fodors.com.

Restaurants

Unless we state otherwise, restaurants are open for lunch and dinner daily. We mention dress code only when there's a specific requirement and reservations only when they're essential or not accepted. To make restaurant reservations, visit Fodors.com.

Credit Cards

The hotels and restaurants in this guide typically accept credit cards. If not, we'll say so.

Top Picks
★ Fodor'sChoice

Listings
⊠ Address
⊠ Branch address
🕼 Mailing address
🖀 Telephone
🖦 Fax
⊕ Website
✇ E-mail

🕮 Admission fee
🕓 Open/closed times
Ⓜ Subway
✛ Directions or Map coordinates

Hotels & Restaurants
🏨 Hotel
🛏 Number of rooms
🍽 Meal plans

✕ Restaurant
🍴 Reservations
🏛 Dress code
🖃 No credit cards
💲 Price

Other
⇨ See also
☞ Take note
⛳ Golf facilities

EXPERIENCE
ARUBA

WHAT'S WHERE

1 Palm Beach. Aruba's biggest high-rise hotels are located along Palm Beach, which is one of the island's best swimming beaches, with calm water. You'll have your widest choice of big resorts, restaurants, casinos, and watersports here, but this is a busy place, so don't go here to escape from the crowds.

2 Eagle Beach. Aruba's so-called "low-rise" hotel area is lined with smaller boutique resorts and, increasingly, time-share resorts. Still, Eagle Beach is wider than Palm Beach, so it's not as crowded, and it's the island's best big beach.

3 Manchebo Beach. Just south of Eagle Beach, Manchebo has rougher surf, but it's rarely as crowded and has many fewer resorts. The beach here flows directly into Druif Beach, which is dominated by the sprawling Divi resort complex.

4 Oranjestad. Aruba's capital is a great place to go for shopping, restaurants, and nightlife or to make arrangements for a tour or other activity. Although there are a few hotels here, including the beautiful Renaissance Aruba, the city has no beachfront.

KEY

Beaches

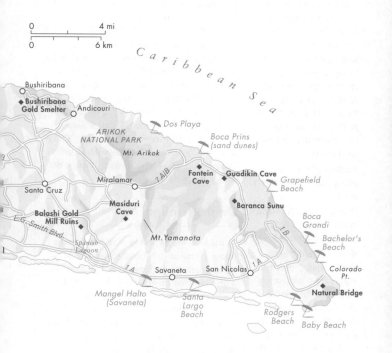

0 4 mi
0 6 km

C a r i b b e a n   S e a

Bushiribana
◆ **Bushiribana
Gold Smelter** Andicouri

Dos Playa

*ARIKOK
NATIONAL PARK*

*Boca Prins
(sand dunes)*

Mt. Arikok

Miralamar   *7 A/B*   ◆ **Fontein
Cave**   **Guadikin Cave**

Santa Cruz   *Grapefield
Beach*

**Masiduri
Cave** ◆   **Baranca Sunu** ◆

**Balashi Gold
Mill Ruins** ◆   *Boca
Grandi*

L.G. Smith Blvd.   *Spanish
Lagoon*   Mt. Yamanota   *1 B*   *Bachelor's
Beach*

1 A   Savaneta   San Nicolas   *1 A*   *Colorado
Pt.*

Natural Bridge ◆

*Mangel Halto
(Savaneta)*   *Santa
Largo
Beach*   *Rodgers
Beach*   *Baby Beach*

PLANNER

Island Activities

Since soft, sandy **beaches** and turquoise waters are the biggest draws in Aruba, they can be crowded. Eagle Beach is the best the island has to offer.

Aruba also comes alive by night, and has become a true **party hot spot**. The casinos—though not as elaborate as those in Las Vegas—are among the best of any Caribbean island.

Restaurants can be pricey, but many are very good.

Diving is good in Aruba, though perhaps not as great as in Bonaire.

Near-constant breezes and tranquil, protected waters have proven to be a boon for **windsurfers,** who have discovered that conditions on the southwestern coast are ideal for their sport.

A largely undeveloped region in Arikok National Wildlife Park is the destination of choice for visitors wishing to **hike** and explore some wild terrain.

Logistics

Getting to Aruba: Aruba is 2½ hours from Miami and 4½ hours from New York. Smaller airlines connect the Dutch islands in the Caribbean, often using Aruba as a hub. Travelers to the U.S. clear Customs and Immigration before leaving Aruba.

Nonstops: There are nonstop flights from Atlanta (Delta), Boston (American, JetBlue, US Airways), Charlotte (US Airways), Chicago (United—weekly), Fort Lauderdale (Spirit—weekly), Houston (Continental—weekly), Miami (American), Newark (Continental), New York–JFK (American, Delta, JetBlue), New York–LGA (Continental—weekly), Philadelphia (US Airways—twice-weekly), and Washington, DC–Dulles (United), though not all flights are daily.

On the Ground

A taxi from the airport to most hotels takes about 20 minutes. It'll cost about $22 to get to the hotels along Eagle Beach, $25 to the high-rise hotels on Palm Beach, and $18 to the hotels downtown. Buses are also an option for traveling around the island, and are especially convenient for shorter trips. Buses only run once an hour, but the price is right, at $1.25 one-way ($2.25 round-trip).

Renting a Car: Rent a car to explore independently, but for just getting to and around town taxis are preferable, and you can use tour companies to arrange your activities. Rent a four-wheel-drive vehicle if you plan to explore the island's natural sights.

Dining and Lodging on Aruba

Aruba is known for its large, luxurious high-rise resorts and vast array of time-shares. But the island also has a nice selection of smaller, low-rise resorts for travelers who don't want to feel lost in a large, impersonal hotel complex. If you're on a budget, consider booking one of the island's many apartment-style units, so you can eat in sometimes instead of having to rely on restaurants exclusively.

Since the all-inclusive resort scheme hasn't taken over Aruba, as it has many other islands, you'll find a wide range of good independent and resort-based restaurant choices. There's a variety of restaurants in Oranjestad, the island's capital, but you'll also find good choices in the resort areas of Eagle and Palm beaches, as well as Savaneta and San Nicolas.

Hotel and Restaurant Costs

Prices in the restaurant reviews are the average cost of a main course at dinner or, if dinner isn't served, at lunch; taxes and service charges are generally included. Prices in the hotel reviews are the lowest cost of a standard double room in high season, excluding taxes, service charges, and meal plans (except at all-inclusives). Prices for rentals are the lowest per-night cost for a one-bedroom unit in high season.

Tips for Travelers

Currency: You probably won't need to change any money if you're coming from the U.S. American currency is accepted almost everywhere in Aruba, though you might get some change back in local currency—the Aruban florin, also called the guilder.

Electricity: 110 volts, just as in the U.S.

Nightlife: Aruba is renowned for its nightlife and casinos; the legal drinking and gambling age is 18.

Traffic: Oranjestad traffic can be heavy during rush hour. Allow a bit of extra time if you're trying to get into town for dinner.

Water: You can safely drink the water in Aruba, but you may not want to. Almost all of the island's water is desalinated seawater, and you may find it tastes flat.

WHEN TO GO

Aruba's high season runs from early December through mid-April. During this season you're guaranteed the most entertainment at resorts and the most people with whom to enjoy it. It's also the most fashionable and most expensive time to visit, both for people staying a week or more and for cruise-ship passengers coming ashore. During this period hotels are solidly booked, and you must make reservations at least two or three months in advance for the very best places (and to get the best airfares). During the rest of the year hotel prices can drop 20% to 40% after April 15.

Climate

Aruba doesn't really have a rainy season and rarely sees a hurricane—one reason why the island is more popular than most during the off-season from mid-May through mid-November, when the risk of Atlantic hurricanes is at its highest. Temperatures are constant (along with the trade winds) year-round. Expect daytime temperatures in the 80s Fahrenheit and nighttime temperatures in the high 70s year-round.

Festivals and Events

January–March: Carnival. Weeks of parties and cultural events precede this two-day street party in late February or early March.

May: Aruba Soul Beach Music Festival. This concert features international artists and takes place over two days on Memorial Day weekend at a different resort every year. ⊕ *www.soulbeach.net*

July: Aruba Hi-Winds. This wind- and kite-surf event takes place over six days, usually in late June or early July. It brings windsurfers of all skill levels from more than 30 different countries to compete off the beaches at Fisherman's Huts at Hadikurari and is considered by some to be the best in the Caribbean. ⊕ *www.hiwindsaruba.com*

August: Aruba Regatta. Three days of racing and parties, this is one of Aruba's annual highlights. ⊕ *www.aruba-regatta.com*

October: Caribbean Sea Jazz. A two-day musical extravaganza featuring international and local jazz and pop performers. ⊕ *www.caribbeanseajazz.com*

November: Aruba in Style. Runway shows, designers, stylists, and cocktail parties make for three days of Aruban glam. ⊕ *www.arubainstyle.com*

Year-round: Bon Bini Festival. Every Tuesday evening Fort Zoutman comes alive with music and local folk dancing.

GREAT ITINERARIES

Are you perplexed about which of Aruba's many beaches is best or about how to spend your time during one of the island's rare rainy days? Below are some suggestions to guide you. There are also a few ideas on how to create a night that completes a perfect day.

A Perfect Day at the Beach

If you didn't bring your own, borrow or rent snorkel gear at your hotel so that you can fully appreciate the calm water and all its inhabitants. Eagle Beach is the island's best, and you can grab a space under one of the many palapa umbrellas if you arrive early enough. The water here is fine for both swimming and snorkeling. Be sure to take in liquids regularly to avoid dehydration—rum punch may sound good, but water is probably best. As the sun goes down, hop back across the road to the very casual Pata Pata Bar at La Cabana Resort for happy hour. There's no need to change.

A Perfect Rainy Day

Even though Aruba is outside the hurricane belt, you may find yourself with a rainy day. Start off with breakfast at Deli-France in the Certified Mega Mall, then head to downtown Oranjestad and visit some museums, perhaps the Archaeological Museum of Aruba or the Numismatic Museum. Then why wait until dinner to have an elegant meal when you can have one for lunch? Make a reservation at L. G. Smith's Steak & Chop House, one of Aruba's best restaurants. After lunch, head to the Mandara Spa at Marriott's Aruba Ocean Club; your body will thank you. Your soul will, too. Or if you want more activity, try the Eagle Bowling Palace. You could also take in a movie at Seaport Cinema in the Seaport Village Mall.

A Perfect Night of Romance

Aruba is one of the most romantic places on earth, and one of Aruba's most romantic experiences is a sunset cruise. Try a voyage on the 43-foot sailing yacht *Tranquilo,* which includes drinks. If you don't have your sea legs yet, a sunset catamaran cruise might be more your style. For dinner, Pinchos Grill & Bar is hard to beat, even on an island filled with romantic dining options. End the evening with a walk—hand in hand—along the waterfront.

ARUBA WITH KIDS

Aruba has a kid-loving culture and their slogan of "One Happy Island" extends to young visitors as well. The island is just a reasonably short flight away from most of the Eastern Seaboard (about 3 to 6 hours), and there are familiar sights such as fast food places that help make kids feel more comfortable. Though the island may not offer all of the distractions of a theme park holiday, it has more than enough to keep most kids occupied during a family vacation.

Where to Stay

Virtually all the best places to stay for families are on or along the beaches that run the length of the western side of the island. The island's east coast is rocky with rough seas and offers little in the way of accommodations. Aruba is a sun-and-sand destination, so most families will find their dollar best spent picking a hotel as close to the beach as their budget will allow. An ocean view isn't a necessity but ease of access to one of the beaches is recommended.

Best High-Rise Resorts. Choose a high-rise resort if you want a great variety of amenities and activities. Most of Aruba's high-rise resorts offer kids programs and are generally found along **Palm Beach**. The **Westin Aruba** has a terrific kids' program that includes a Director of Fun and a program called Love Your Family. It's a large resort, on the beach, with many entertainment options including a popular Magic Live! comedy-magic show. The **Hyatt Regency Aruba Beach Resort** offers an extensive kids' program and has many family-fun activities such as horseback riding, various watersports, and tennis.

Best Low-rise Resorts. Aruba's smaller low-rise properties don't offer as many amenities as the high-rises, but they provide a relaxing, laid-back vibe and some do have kids programs. Low-rise properties are mostly found along **Eagle Beach, Manchebo Beach, and Druif Beach** and are often less crowded. **Amsterdam Manor** on Eagle Beach is a good value-hotel with kitchenettes and a mini-grocery store on-site so families can save money and enjoy a relaxing stay. At **Divi Aruba All-Inclusive** on Druif Beach, children under 18 stay free when accompanied by two adults, and their kids' camp even offers Papiamento language lessons. The beach here is gorgeous and nonmotorized watersports are all included in the price.

Beaches

Palm Beach is wide and offers powdery white sand, generally calm waters, and plenty of nearby amenities like food and beverages. Families that want a bit more room to move around away from the crowds might find **Druif** and **Manchebo** beaches more to their liking but there aren't as many options for chair rentals and refreshments. Sprawling **Eagle Beach** offers the best of all worlds with fewer crowds and a range of amenities within easy walking distance.

Water Activities

Snorkeling, swimming, kayaking, and sailing are some of the things that keep families coming back to Aruba year after year. Most hotels and condos offer inexpensive equipment rentals for a day in the water. Seasoned junior snorkelers will find the viewing pretty dull off the major beaches, so organized tours such as those offered by **De Palm Tours** and **Red Sail Sports**, which explore more remote coves, may provide more of a satisfying underwater experience. **De Palm Island** offers a variety of water activities for kids including excellent snorkeling and a water park that makes for a great day in the sun.

Though a bit pricey for larger families the **Atlantis Submarine Tour** will likely entertain even the most jaded teen.

Land Activities

The **Aruba Ostrich Farm** is an excellent short excursion that can entertain young kids while not boring adults to tears. **The Butterfly Farm** is convenient and probably worth a visit for an hour or so, but older kids may find the pace a bit slow and overly educational.

Families looking more adventure and encounters with local wildlife can try a day of hiking at **Arikok National Park.** Eddy Croes of **Aruba Nature Sensitive Tours** is a former ranger at the park and will turn the excursion into a fun learning experience.

EXPLORING

BALMY SUNSHINE, SILKY SAND, aquamarine waters, natural scenic wonders, outstanding dining, decent shopping, and an array of nightly entertainment . . . Aruba's got it in spades. It's also unusual in its range of choices, from world-class oceanfront resorts equipped with gourmet restaurants and high-dollar casinos to intimate neighborhood motels and diners not far off the beach.

Aruba's wildly sculpted landscape is replete with rocky deserts, cactus clusters, secluded coves, blue vistas, and the trademark divi-divi tree. To preserve the environment while encouraging visitors to explore, the government has implemented an ongoing ecotourism plan. Initiatives include finding ways to make efficient use of the limited land resources and protecting the natural and cultural resources in such preserves as Arikok National Park and the Coastal Protection Zone (along the island's north and east coasts).

Oranjestad, Aruba's capital, is good for shopping by day and dining by night, but the "real Aruba"—with its untamed beauty—is discovered in the countryside. Rent a car, take a sightseeing tour, or hire a cab by the hour to explore. Though remote, the northern and eastern shores are striking and well worth a visit. A drive out past the California Lighthouse or to Seroe Colorado will give you a feel for the backcountry.

The main highways are well paved, but the windward side of the island has some roads that are a mixture of compacted dirt and stones. A car is fine, but a four-wheel-drive vehicle will enable you to better navigate the unpaved interior. Remember that few beaches outside the hotel strip along Palm and Eagle beaches to the west have refreshment stands, so pack your own food and drinks. Aside from those in the infrequent restaurant, there are no public bathrooms outside of Oranjestad.

Traffic is sparse, but signs leading to sights are often small and hand-lettered (this is slowly changing as the government puts up official road signs), so watch closely. Route 1A travels southbound along the western coast, and 1B is simply northbound along the same road. If you lose your way, just follow the divi-divi trees.

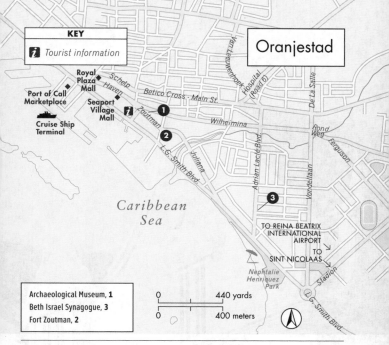

KEY

🛈 Tourist information

Oranjestad

Royal Plaza Mall
Port of Call Marketplace
Schelp Haven
Betico Cross - Main St
Seaport Village Mall
Cruise Ship Terminal
Zoutman
Wilhelmina
L.G. Smith Blvd
Juliana
Adrian Lacle Blvd
Van Leeuwenhoek
Hospital (Road 6)
De La Salle
Rond Weg
Vondellaan
Ferguson

Caribbean Sea

TO REINA BEATRIX INTERNATIONAL AIRPORT
TO SINT NICOLAAS
Nephtalie Henriquez Park
Stadion
L.G. Smith Blvd

Archaeological Museum, **1**
Beth Israel Synagogue, **3**
Fort Zoutman, **2**

0 ———— 440 yards
0 ———— 400 meters

ORANJESTAD AND ENVIRONS

Aruba's capital is best explored on foot. Its palm-lined central thoroughfare runs between old and new pastel-painted buildings of typical Dutch design (Spanish influence is also evident in some of the architecture). There are many malls with boutiques and shops; downtown and Seaport Village are the major shopping areas. Every morning the wharf teems with activity as merchants sell produce and fresh fish—often right off their boats. You can also buy handicrafts and T-shirts at this dockside bazaar, where bargaining is expected and dollars or florins are accepted. Island schooners and houseboats anchored near the fishing boats add to the port's ambience. Wilhelmina Park, a small tropical garden on the waterfront along L.G. Smith Boulevard, has a sculpture of the Netherlands' Queen Wilhelmina, who reigned from 1890 to 1948.

TIMING

There's rarely a day when there aren't at least two cruise ships docked in Oranjestad, so the downtown shopping area is usually bustling. Some of the smaller stores are closed Sunday, but virtually all the larger ones are open to accommodate cruise passengers looking for bargains. When there are more than two ships in port, expect lines at retail outlets and long waits at restaurants.

TOP ATTRACTIONS

FAMILY **Archaeological Museum of Aruba.** This small museum has two rooms chock-full of fascinating artifacts from the indigenous Arawak people, including farm and domestic utensils dating back hundreds of years. ⊠ *J.E. Irausquin Blvd. 2A* ☏ *297/582–8979* ⚑ *Free* ☉ *Tues.–Sun. 10–5.*

Aruba Aloe. Learn all about aloe—its cultivation, processing, and production—at this farm and factory. Guided tours lasting about a half hour will show you how the gel—revered for its skin-soothing properties—is extracted from the aloe vera plant and used in a variety of products, including after-sun creams, soaps, and shampoos. Though not the most exciting tour on the island—and unlikely to keeps kids entertained—it is free and might be a good option on a rainy day. You can purchase the finished goods in the gift shop where the tour ends. ⊠ *Pitastraat 115* ☏ *297/588–3222* ⚑ *Free* ☉ *Weekdays 8:30–4, Sat. 9–noon.*

Balashi Brewery. The factory that manufactures the excellent local beer, Balashi, offers daily tours that will take you through every stage of the brewing process. It makes for a fascinating hour, and the price of the tour includes a free drink at the end. Closed shoes are required for the tour. Those more interested in beer drinking than beer making might want to visit the factory Friday evening from 6 to 9 for happy hour, when there's live music. ⊠ *Balashi 75, Balashi* ☏ *297/592–2544* ⊕ *www.balashi.com* ⚑ *$6.*

WORTH NOTING

Beth Israel Synagogue. Built in 1962, this synagogue is the only Jewish house of worship on Aruba, and it strives to meet the needs of its Ashkenazi, Sephardic, European, North American, and South American worshippers. The island's Jewish community dates back to the opening of the oil refinery in the 1920s, when small congregations gathered in private homes in San Nicolas. The temple holds regular services on Friday at 8 pm and on Saturday at 8 pm; additional services are held on high holy days.

CLOSE UP

Papiamento Primer

Papiamento is a hybrid language born out of the colorful past of Aruba, Bonaire, and Curaçao. The language's use is generally thought to have started in the 17th century when Sephardic Jews migrated with their African slaves from Brazil to Curaçao. The slaves spoke a pidgin Portuguese, which may have been blended with pure Portuguese, some Dutch (the colonial power in charge of the island), and Arawakan. Proximity to the mainland meant that Spanish and English words were also incorporated.

Papiamento is roughly translated as "the way of speaking." (Sometimes the suffix *-mentu* is spelled in the Spanish and Portuguese way [*-mento*], creating the variant spelling.) It began as an oral tradition, handed down through the generations and spoken by all social classes on the islands. There's no uniform spelling or grammar from island to island, or even from one neighborhood to another. However, it's beginning to receive some official recognition. A noteworthy measure of the increased government respect for the language is that anyone applying for citizenship must be fluent in both Papiamento and Dutch.

Arubans enjoy it when visitors use their language, so don't be shy. You can buy a Papiamento dictionary to build your vocabulary, but here are a few pleasantries to get you started:

Bon dia. Good morning.

Bon tardi. Good afternoon.

Bon nochi. Good evening/night.

Bon bini. Welcome.

Ajo. Bye.

Te aworo. See you later.

Pasa un bon dia. Have a good day.

Danki. Thank you.

Na bo ordo. You're welcome.

Con ta bai? How are you?

Mi ta bon. I am fine.

Ban goza! Let's enjoy!

Pabien! Congratulations!

Quanto costa esaki? How much is this?

Hopi bon. Very good.

Ami. Me.

Abo. You.

Nos dos. The two of us.

Mi dushi. My sweetheart.

Ku tur mi amor. With all my love.

Un braza. A hug.

Un sunchi. A kiss.

Mi stima Aruba. I love Aruba.

Visitors are always welcome, although it's best to make an appointment to see the synagogue when there's not a service. A Judaica shop sells keepsakes, kosher dry goods, and kiddush wines. ⊠ *Adrian Laclé Blvd. 2* ☎ *297/582–3272* 🖃 *Free except high holy days.*

Ft. Zoutman. One of the island's oldest edifices, Aruba's historic fort was built in 1796 and played an important role in skirmishes between British and Curaçao troops in 1803. The Willem III Tower, named for the Dutch monarch of that time, was added in 1868 to serve as a lighthouse. Over time the fort has been a government office building, a police station, and a prison; now its historical museum displays Aruban artifacts in an 18th-century house. ⊠ *Zoutmanstraat* ☎ *297/582–6099* 🖃 *Free* ⊘ *Weekdays 8–noon and 1–4.*

MANCHEBO AND DRUIF BEACHES

One beach seamlessly merges with another resulting in a miles-long stretch of powdery sand peppered with a few low-rise resorts. This part of the island is much less crowded than Palm Beach and great for a morning or evening stroll.

EAGLE BEACH

This area is often referred to as Aruba's low-rise hotel area. It's lined with smaller boutique resorts and time-share resorts. Eagle Beach is considered one of the best beaches in the Caribbean, the white sand here seems to stretch on forever. The water is great for swimming and there are numerous refreshment spots along the beach. Although the beach can get busy during the day there's never a problem finding a spot, but if you're looking for shade, it's best to stick near one of the hotel bar huts along the beach.

PALM BEACH AND NOORD

The district of Noord is home to the strip of high-rise hotels and casinos that line Palm Beach. The hotels and restaurants, ranging from haute cuisine to fast food, are densely packed into a few miles running along the beachfront. When other areas of Aruba are shutting down for the night, this area is guaranteed to still be buzzing with activity. Here you can also find the beautiful **St. Ann's Church,** known for its ornate 19th-century altar. In this area Aruban-style homes are scattered amid clusters of cacti.

TOP ATTRACTIONS

FAMILY **Butterfly Farm.** Hundreds of butterflies from around the world flutter about this spectacular garden. Guided 30- to 45-minute tours (included in the price of admission) provide an entertaining look into the life cycle of these insects, from egg to caterpillar to chrysalis to butterfly. After your initial visit, you can return as often as you like for free during your vacation. ⊠ *J.E. Irausquin Blvd., Palm Beach* ☎ *297/586–3656* ⊕ *www.thebutterflyfarm.com* ☞ *$15* ⊘ *Daily 9–4:30; last tour at 4.*

WORTH NOTING

Bubali Bird Sanctuary. More than 80 species of migratory birds nest in this man-made wetland area inland from the island's strip of high-rise hotels. Herons, egrets, cormorants, coots, gulls, skimmers, terns, and ducks are among the winged wonders in and around the two interconnected artificial lakes that make up the sanctuary. ⊠ *J.E. Irausquin Blvd., Noord* ☞ *Free.*

WESTERN TIP (CALIFORNIA DUNES)

No trip to Aruba is complete without a visit to the California Lighthouse and it's also worth exploring the rugged area of the Island's Western tip. This is the transition point between Aruba's calmer and rougher coasts. Malmok Beach and Arashi Beach are popular for windsurfing and are excellent for grabbing dramatic sunset photos.

TOP ATTRACTIONS

California Lighthouse. The lighthouse, built by a French architect in 1910, stands at the island's far northern end. Although you can't go inside, you can climb the hill to the lighthouse base for some great views. It's surrounded by huge boulders and sand dunes; in this stark landscape you might feel as though you've just landed on the moon. ⊠ *Arashi.*

WORTH NOTING

Alto Vista Chapel. Alone near the island's northwest corner sits this scenic little chapel. The wind whistles through the simple mustard-color walls, eerie boulders, and looming cacti. Along the side of the road back to civilization are miniature crosses with depictions of the stations of the cross and hand-lettered signs with "Pray for us Sinners" and other heartfelt evocations of faith. ⊠ *Alto Vista Rd.* ✛ *Follow the rough, winding dirt road that loops around the island's northern tip, or from the hotel strip, take Palm Beach Road through three intersections and watch for the asphalt road to the left just past the Alto Vista Rum Shop.*

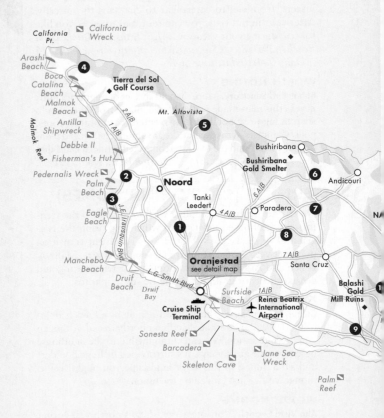

Aruba

California
Pt.
California
Wreck

Arashi
Beach
Boca
Catalina
Beach
Malmok
Beach

④

**Tierra del Sol
Golf Course**

Antilla
Shipwreck

Malmok Reef

Debbie II

Fisherman's Hut

Pedernalis Wreck

2 A/B

1 A/B

Mt. Altovista

⑤

Bushiribana ◯

**Bushiribana
Gold Smelter**

Andicouri ◯

⑥

②

Palm
Beach

③

Eagle
Beach

Noord ◯

Tanki
Leedert ◯

4 A/B

6 A/B

Paradera ◯

⑦

①

⑧

NA

J.E. Irausquin Blvd.

Manchebo
Beach

Druif
Beach

Druif
Bay

L.G. Smith Blvd.

Oranjestad
see detail map

Surfside
Beach

7 A/B

Santa Cruz ◯

**Balashi
Gold
Mill Ruins**

①

**Cruise Ship
Terminal**

1 A/B

**Reina Beatrix
International
Airport** ✈

Sonesta Reef

Barcadera

Skeleton Cave

Jane Sea
Wreck

Palm
Reef

⑨

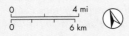

0   4 mi
0   6 km

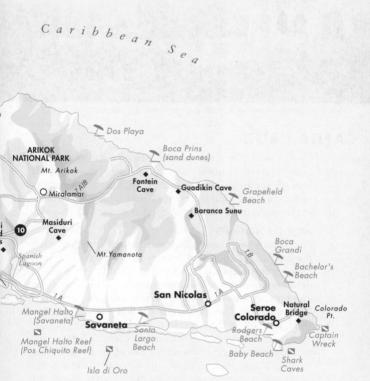

Alto Vista Chapel, **5**	Butterfly Farm, **2**
Aruba Aloe, **1**	California Lighthouse, **4**
Aruba Ostrich Farm, **6**	Frenchman's Pass, **10**
Balashi Brewery, **9**	Mt. Hooiberg, **8**
Bubali Bird Sanctuary, **3**	Rock Formations, **7**

C a r i b b e a n   S e a

Dos Playa

Boca Prins
(sand dunes)

ARIKOK NATIONAL PARK
Mt. Arikok

O Miralamar

Fontein Cave

Guadikin Cave

Grapefield Beach

Baranca Sunu

Masiduri Cave

10

Spanish Lagoon

Mt. Yamanota

Boca Grandi

Bachelor's Beach

1B

San Nicolas   *1A*

Seroe Colorado

Natural Bridge

Colorado Pt.

1A

Mangel Halto (Savaneta)

Savaneta

Santa Largo Beach

Rodgers Beach

Captain Wreck

Mangel Halto Reef (Pos Chiquito Reef)

Baby Beach

Shark Caves

Isla di Oro

KEY	
Beaches	
Dive Sites	

Alto Vista Chapel, on the windy northwest coast of Aruba, was built in 1750.

SANTA CRUZ

Though not a tourist hot spot (by Aruba standards) this town in the center of the island offers a good taste of how the locals live. It's not architecturally interesting, but there are many restaurants and local shops offering something a bit different from the usual tourist fare (and at reasonable prices).

WORTH NOTING

Frenchman's Pass. Overhanging trees and towering cacti border this luscious stretch of road. The pass is almost midway between Oranjestad and San Nicolas; follow L.G. Smith Boulevard past a shimmering vista of blue-green sea and turn off where you see the drive-in theater (a popular local hangout). Then proceed to the first intersection, turn right, and follow the curve to the right. Gold was discovered on Aruba in 1824, and near Frenchman's Pass are the massive concrete-and-limestone ruins of the **Balashi Gold Smelter,** a nice place to picnic and listen to the chattering parakeets. A magnificent, gnarled divi-divi tree guards the entrance. The area now is home to Aruba's desalination plant, where all of the island's drinking water is purified.

Mt. Hooiberg. Named for its shape (*hooiberg* means "haystack" in Dutch), this 541-foot peak lies inland just past the airport. If you have the energy, you can climb the 562 steps to the top for an impressive view of Oranjestad (and Venezuela on clear days).

A ...OD TOUR

Weste... ...ba is where you'll likely spend most of your time. All the resorts and time-shares are along this coast, most of them clustered on the oceanfront strip at the luscious Palm and Eagle beaches, in the city of Oranjestad, or in the district of Noord. All the casinos, major shopping malls, and most restaurants are found in this region, as is the airport.

Rent a car and head out on Route 1A toward **Oranjestad** for some sightseeing and shopping. Pick up Route 1B out of town. At a large roundabout turn right and drive for about 1 km (½ mile), then make another right at the first intersection and drive for ½ km (¼ mile) until you reach the fields and factory of **Aruba Aloe**. Head back to the roundabout and pick up Route 4A. Follow this road a short way to the **Ayo and Casibari Rock Formations**. Continue on 4A and follow the signs for **Hooiberg**; if you're so inclined, climb the steps of

Haystack Hill. Return on 4B to 6A and drive a couple of miles to the Bushiribana Gold Smelter. Beyond it on the windward coast is the **Aruba Ostrich Farm**.

From here, take 6B to the intersection of Route 3B, which you'll follow into the town of **Noord**, a good place to stop for lunch. Then take Route 2B, following the signs for the branch road leading to the **Alto Vista Chapel**. Return to town and pick up 2B and then 1B to reach the **California Lighthouse**. In this area you can also see Arashi Beach (a popular snorkeling site) and the Tierra del Sol golf course. From the lighthouse, follow 1A back toward Palm Beach. On the way, stop at the **Butterfly Farm** and the **Bubali Bird Sanctuary**.

...n just about complete the above tour in one very full day. If you want to linger in Oranjestad's shops or go snorkeling along the beach, consider breaking the tour up into two days.

SAVANETA

The Dutch settled here after retaking the island in 1816, and it served as Aruba's first capital. Today it's a bustling fishing village with a 150-year-old *cas di torto* (mud hut), the oldest dwelling still standing on the island.

DID YOU KNOW?

Unlike the idyllic beaches of the south and west, Aruba's northeast coast, which faces the open Caribbean, is pounded by fierce waves pushed inland from near-constant trade winds.

The Divi-Divi Tree

Like a statuesque dancer in a graceful flat-back pose, the *watapana*, or divi-divi tree, is one of Aruba's hallmarks. Oddly enough, this tropical shrub is a member of the legume family. Its astringent pods contain high levels of tannin, which is leached out for tanning leather. The pods also yield a black dye. The tree has a moderate rate of growth and a high drought tolerance. Typically it reaches no more than 25 feet in height, with a flattened crown and irregular, forked branches. Its leaves are dull green, and its inconspicuous yet fragrant flowers are pale yellow or white and grow in small clusters. Thanks to constant trade winds, the divi-divis serve as a natural compass: they're bent toward the island's leeward—or western—side, where most of the hotels are.

SAN NICOLAS

During the oil refinery heyday, Aruba's oldest village was a bustling port; now its primary purpose is tourism. The major institution in town is Charlie's Restaurant & Bar. Stop in for a drink and advice on what to see and do in this little town. Aruba's main red-light district is here and will be fairly apparent to even casual observers.

SEROE COLORADO

What was originally built as a community for oil workers is known for its intriguing 1939 chapel. The site is surreal, as organ-pipe cacti form the backdrop for sedate white-washed cottages. The real reason to come here is a **natural bridge.** Keep bearing east past the community, continuing uphill until you run out of road. You can then hike down to the cathedral-like formation. It's not too strenuous, but watch your footing as you descend. Be sure to follow the white arrows painted on the rocks, as there are no other directional signs. Although this bridge isn't as spectacular as its more celebrated sibling (which collapsed in 2005), the raw elemental power of the sea that created it, replete with hissing blowholes, certainly is.

Aruba's divi-divi trees are always bent toward the west, where you'll find the best beaches.

ARIKOK NATIONAL PARK AND ENVIRONS

Nearly 20% of Aruba has been designated part of Arikok National Park, which sprawls across the eastern interior and the northeast coast. The park is the keystone of the government's long-term ecotourism plan to preserve Aruba's resources and showcases the island's flora and fauna as well as ancient Arawak petroglyphs, the ruins of a gold-mining operation at Miralmar, and the remnants of Dutch peasant settlements at Masiduri. Within the confines of the park are Mt. Arikok and the 620-foot Mt. Yamanota, Aruba's highest peak.

Anyone looking for geological exotica should head for the park's caves, found on the northeastern coast. Baranca Sunu, the so-called Tunnel of Love, has a heart-shaped entrance and naturally sculpted rocks farther inside that look like the Madonna, Abraham Lincoln, and even a jaguar. Fontein Cave, which was used by indigenous peoples centuries ago, is marked with ancient drawings (rangers are on hand to offer explanations). Bats are known to make appearances—don't worry, they won't bother you. Although you don't need a flashlight because the paths are well lighted, it's best to wear sneakers.

A GOOD TOUR

Take Route 1A to Route 4B and visit the Balashi Gold Smelter ruins and **Frenchman's Pass**. Return to 1A and continue your drive past Mangel Halto Beach to **Savaneta**, a fishing village and one of several residential areas that have examples of typical Aruban homes. Follow 1A to **San Nicolas**, where you can meander along the main promenade, pick up a few souvenirs, and grab a bite to eat. Heading out of town, continue on 1A until you hit a fork in the road; follow the signs toward **Seroe Colorado**, with the nearby natural bridge and the Colorado Point Lighthouse. From here, follow the signs toward Rodgers Beach, just one of several area shores where you can kick back for a while. Nearby Baby Beach, with calm waters and beautiful white sand, is a favorite spot for snorkelers. To the north, on Route 7B, is Boca Grandi, a great windsurfing spot. Next is Grapefield Beach, a stretch of white sand that glistens against a backdrop of cliffs and boulder formations. Shortly beyond it, on 7B, you'll come into **Arikok National Park**, where you can explore caves and tunnels, play on sand dunes, and tackle Mt. Yamanota, Aruba's highest elevation. Farther along 7B is **Santa Cruz**, where a wooden cross stands atop a hill to mark the spot where Christianity was introduced to the islanders. The same highway will bring you all the way into Oranjestad.

TIMING
You can see most of eastern Aruba's sights in a half day, though it's easy to fill a full day if you spend time relaxing on a sandy beach or exploring the trails in Arikok National Park.

TOP ATTRACTIONS
Arikok Visitor Center. At the park's main entrance, Arikok Visitor Center houses offices, restrooms, and food facilities. All visitors must stop here upon entering so that officials can manage the traffic flow and hand out information on park rules and features. ☎ 297/585–1234 ⊕ www.arubanationalpark.org ☎ $10 ⊙ 8–5.

Aruba Ostrich Farm. Everything you ever wanted to know about the world's largest living birds can be found at this farm. A large *palapa* (palm-thatched roof) houses a gift shop and restaurant that draws large bus tours, and tours of the farm are available every half hour. This operation is virtually identical to the facility in Curaçao; it's owned by

Cunucu Houses

Pastel houses surrounded by cacti fences adorn Aruba's flat, rugged *cunucu* ("country" in Papiamento). The features of these traditional houses were developed in response to the environment. Early settlers discovered that slanting roofs allowed the heat to rise and that small windows helped to keep in the cool air. Among the earliest building materials was *caliche,* a durable calcium-carbonate substance found in the island's southeastern hills.

Many houses were also built using interlocking coral rocks that didn't require mortar (this technique is no longer used, thanks to cement and concrete). Contemporary design combines some of the basic principles of the earlier homes with touches of modernization: windows, though still narrow, have been elongated; roofs are constructed of bright tiles; pretty patios have been added; and doorways and balconies present an ornamental face to the world beyond.

the same company. ✉ *Makividiri Rd., Paradera* ☎ *297/585–9630* ⊕ *www.arubaostrichfarm.com* 💰 *Adults $12, children under 12 $6* ⊙ *Daily 9–4.*

Rock Formations. The massive boulders at Ayo and Casibari are a mystery, as they don't match the island's geological makeup. You can climb to the top for fine views of the arid countryside. On the way you'll doubtless pass Aruba whiptail lizards—the males are cobalt blue, and the females are blue-gray with light-blue dots. The main path to Casi-

bari has steps and handrails, and you must move through tunnels and along narrow steps and ledges to reach the top. At Ayo you can find ancient pictographs in a small cave (the entrance has iron bars to protect the drawings from vandalism). You may also encounter boulder climbers, who are increasingly drawn to Ayo's smooth surfaces. ⊠ *Paradera* ✛ *Access to the rock formations at Casibari is via Tanki Highway 4A; you can reach Ayo via Route 6A. Watch carefully for the turnoff signs near the center of the island on the way to the windward side.*

3

BEACHES

THE BEACHES ON ARUBA ARE LEGENDARY: white sand, turquoise waters, and virtually no litter—everyone takes the *"No Tira Sushi"* (no littering) signs very seriously, especially considering the island's $280 fine. The major public beaches, which back up to the hotels along the southwestern strip, are usually crowded. You can make the hour-long hike from the Holiday Inn to the Tamarijn without ever leaving sand. Make sure you're well protected from the sun—it scorches fast despite the cooling trade winds. Luckily, there's at least one covered bar (and often an ice-cream stand) at virtually every hotel. On the island's northeastern side stronger winds make the waters too choppy for swimming, but the vistas are great and the terrain is wonderful for exploring.

Arashi Beach. This is a 1-km (½-mi) stretch of gleaming white sand. Although it was once rocky, nature—with a little help from humans—has turned it into an excellent place for sunbathing and swimming. Despite calm waters, the rocky reputation keeps most people away, making it relatively uncrowded. **Amenities:** parking. **Best for:** swimming; walking. ✉ *West of Malmok Beach, on west end.*

FAMILY **Baby Beach.** On the island's eastern tip (near the refinery), this semicircular beach borders a placid bay that's just about as shallow as a wading pool—perfect for tots, shore divers, and terrible swimmers. Thatched shaded areas are good places to cool off. Down the road is the island's rather unusual pet cemetery. Stop by the nearby snack truck for burgers, hot dogs, beer, and soda. The road to this beach (and several others) is through San Nicolas and along the road toward Seroe Colorado. Just before reaching the beach, keep an eye out for a strange 300-foot natural seawall made of coral and rock that was thrown up overnight when Hurricane Ivan swept by the island in 2004. **Amenities:** food and drink. **Best for:** snorkeling; swimming; walking. ✉ *Near Seroe Colorado, on east end.*

Boca Catalina. Although there are some stones and pebbles along this white-sand beach, snorkelers come for the shallow water filled with fish. Swimmers will also appreciate the calm conditions. There aren't any facilities nearby, however, so pack provisions. **Amenities:** none. **Best for:** snorkeling; swimming; walking. ✉ *Between Arashi Beach and Malmok Beach, north of intersection of 1B and 2B.*

Baby Beach is a great spot for the family.

Boca Grandi. This is a great spot for windsurfers, but swimming is not advisable as the water is rough and there are no lifeguards. It's near Seagrape Grove and the Aruba Golf Club, toward the island's eastern tip. **Amenities:** none. **Best for:** walking; windsurfing. ⊠ *Near Seagrape Grove, on east end.*

Boca Prins. You'll need a four-wheel-drive vehicle to make the trek to this strip of coastline, which is famous for its backdrop of enormous vanilla sand dunes. Near the Fontein Cave and Blue Lagoon, the beach itself is about as large as a Brazilian bikini—but with two rocky cliffs and tumultuously crashing waves, it's as romantic as Aruba gets. The water is rough, and swimming is prohibited. Bring a picnic, a beach blanket, and sturdy sneakers, and descend the rocks that form steps to the water's edge. **Amenities:** none. **Best for:** solitude; walking. ⊠ *Off 7 A/B, near Fontein Cave.*

Bachelor's Beach (*Boca Tabla*). This east-side beach is known for its white-powder sand. The conditions aren't the best for swimming, however. **Amenities:** none. **Best for:** snorkeling; windsurfing. ⊠ *East end, south of Boca Grandi.*

Dos Playa. Hire a four-wheel-drive vehicle, pack a blanket and a picnic basket, and head here to take in the beautiful view. Swimming is discouraged because of strong currents

DID YOU KNOW?

Although the Renaissance Aruba Beach Resort & Casino is in downtown Oranjestad, its private, 40-acre island is reachable by complimentary launches that leave right from the lobby of the Marina Hotel.

and massive waves. **Amenities:** none. **Best for:** walking; solitude. ⊠ *Arikok National Park, just north of Boca Prins.*

Druif Beach. Fine white sand and calm water make this beach a fine choice for sunbathing and swimming. Convenience is a highlight, too: the many Divi hotels are close at hand, and the beach is accessible by bus, rental car, or taxi. **Amenities:** parking. **Best for:** swimming. ⊠ *Parallel to J.E. Irausquin Blvd., near Divi resorts, south of Punta Brabo.*

★ **Fodor's Choice Eagle Beach.** On the southwestern coast, across the highway from what is quickly becoming known as Time-Share Lane, is one of the Caribbean's—if not the world's—best beaches. With all the resorts here, this mile-plus-long beach is always hopping. The white sand is literally dazzling, and sunglasses are essential. Many of the hotels have facilities on or near the beach, and refreshments are never far away. **Amenities:** food and drink; toilets. **Best for:** swimming; walking; sunset. ⊠ *J.E. Irausquin Blvd., north of Manchebo Beach.*

Fisherman's Huts (*Hadicurari*). North of the Marriott is a windsurfer's haven with good swimming conditions and a decent, slightly rocky, white-sand beach. Take a picnic lunch (tables are available) and watch the elegant purple, aqua, and orange sails struggle in the wind. **Amenities:** none. **Best for:** swimming; windsurfing. ⊠ *North of Aruba Marriott Resort, Palm Beach.*

Grapefield Beach. North of Boca Grandi on the Eastern coast, a sweep of blinding-white sand in the shadow of cliffs and boulders is marked by an anchor-shaped memorial dedicated to seamen. Pick sea grapes from January to June. Swim at your own risk; the waves here can be rough. This is not a popular tourist beach, so finding a quiet spot is almost guaranteed, but the downside of this is a complete lack of facilities or nearby refreshments. **Amenities:** none. **Best for:** solitude. ⊠ *Southwest of San Nicolas, on east end.*

Malmok Beach (*Boca Catalina*). On the northwestern shore, this small, nondescript beach borders shallow waters that stretch 300 yards from shore. There are no snack or refreshment stands here, but shade is available under the thatched umbrellas. It's the perfect place to learn to windsurf. Right off the coast here is a favorite haunt for divers and snorkelers—the wreck of the German ship *Antilla*, scuttled in 1940. **Amenities:** none. **Best for:** solitude; snorkeling. ⊠ *At end of J.E. Irausquin Blvd., Malmokweg.*

Manchebo Beach (*Punta Brabo*). Impressively wide, the white sand shoreline in front of the Manchebo Beach Resort is where officials turn a blind eye to the occasional topless sunbather. This beach merges with Druif Beach, and most locals use the name Manchebo to refer to both. **Amenities:** food and drink; toilets. **Best for:** swimming. ✉ *J.E. Irausquin Blvd., at Manchebo Beach Resort.*

Mangel Halto (*Savaneta*). Drive or cab it over to this south-western beach for a lovely setting for a picnic. Hop into the shallow waters for a swim after taking in the sun on the fine white sand. **Amenities:** none. **Best for:** swimming. ✉ *Between Savaneta and Pos Chiquito, San Nicolas.*

Palm Beach. This stretch runs from the Westin Aruba Resort, Spa & Casino to the Marriott's Aruba Ocean Club. It's the center of Aruban tourism, offering good swimming, sailing, and other watersports. In some spots you might find a variety of shells that are great to collect, but not as much fun to step on barefoot—bring sandals. **Amenities:** food and drink; toilets; watersports. **Best for:** swimming; walking. ✉ *J.E. Irausquin Blvd., between Westin Aruba Resort and Marriott's Aruba Ocean Club.*

FAMILY **Rodger's Beach.** Near Baby Beach on the island's eastern tip, this beautiful curving stretch of sand is only slightly marred by its proximity to the oil refinery at the bay's far side. Swimming conditions are excellent here. The snack bar at the water's edge has beach-equipment rentals and a shop. Drive around the refinery perimeter to get here. **Amenities:** food and drink; watersports. **Best for:** swimming. ✉ *Next to Baby Beach, on east end, San Nicolas.*

Santo Largo. Swimming conditions are good—thanks to shallow water edged by white-powder sand—but there are no facilities at this beach west of Mangel Halto. **Amenities:** none. **Best for:** swimming. ✉ *Just west of Savaneta, San Nicolas.*

Surfside. Accessible by public bus, car, or taxi, this beach is the perfect place to swim. It's also conveniently located next to the Havana Beach Club and across the street from the Caribbean Town Beach Resort. **Amenities:** food and drink; parking; toilets. **Best for:** swimming. ✉ *Off L.G. Smith Blvd., just before airport compound, Oranjestad.*

WHERE TO EAT

THERE ARE A FEW HUNDRED RESTAURANTS on Aruba, from elegant eateries to seafront shacks, so you're bound to find something to tantalize your taste buds. You can sample a wide range of cuisines—Italian, French, Argentine, Asian, and Cuban, to name a few—reflecting Aruba's extensive blend of cultures. Chefs have to be creative on this tiny island, because of the limited number of locally grown ingredients: *maripampoen* (a vegetable that's often stewed with meat and potatoes), *hierba di hole* (a sweet-spicy herb used in fish soup), and *shimarucu* (a fruit similar to the cherry) are among the few.

Although most resorts offer better-than-average dining, don't be afraid to try one of the many excellent independent places. Ask locals about their favorite spots; some of the lesser-known restaurants offer food that's reasonably priced and definitely worth sampling.

Most restaurants on the western side of the island are along Palm Beach or in downtown Oranjestad, both easily accessible by taxi or bus. If you're heading to a restaurant in Oranjestad for dinner, leave about 15 minutes earlier than you think you should; in-town traffic can get ugly once beach hours are over. Some restaurants in Savaneta (Flying Fishbone) and San Nicolas (Charlie's Restaurant & Bar) are worth the trip; a car is the best way to get there. Breakfast lovers are in luck. For quantity, check out the buffets at the Hyatt, Marriott, or Westin Aruba Resort, Spa & Casino resorts or local joints such as DeliFrance.

ARUBA DINING PLANNER

ISLAND SAMPLER

Aruba Gastronomic Association (*AGA*). To give visitors an affordable way to sample the island's eclectic cuisine, the Aruba Gastronomic Association has created a Dine-Around program involving more than 20 island restaurants. Here's how it works: you can buy tickets for three dinners ($117 per person), five dinners ($190), seven dinners ($262), or five breakfasts or lunches plus four dinners ($230). Dinners include an appetizer, an entrée, dessert, coffee or tea, and a service charge (except when a restaurant is a "VIP member," in which case $38 will be deducted from your final bill instead). Other programs, such as gift certificates and coupons for dinners at the association's VIP member restaurants, are also available. You can buy Dine-Around tickets using the association's online order form, through

Best Bets for Aruba Dining

With the many restaurants to choose from, how will you decide where to eat? Fodor's writers and editors have selected their favorite restaurants in the Best Bets lists below. The Fodor's Choice properties represent the "best of the best." Find specific details about a restaurant in the full reviews.

Fodor's Choice: Flying Fishbone; Gasparito Restaurant & Art Gallery; Gostoso; Madame Janette's; Marandi; Passions on the Beach; Pinchos Grill & Bar.

Best Budget Eats: Charlie's Restaurant & Bar; Coco Plum; DeliFrance.

Best for Families: Charlie's Restaurant & Bar; El Gaucho Argentine Grill; Hostaria Da' Vittorio.

Most Romantic: Flying Fishbone; Marandi; Papiamento; Passions on the Beach; Pinchos Grill & Bar; Ruinas del Mar; Ventanas del Mar.

Best for Local Aruban Cuisine: Gasparito Restaurant & Art Gallery; Old Cunucu House; Papiamento.

travel agents, or at the De Palm Tours sales desk in many hotels. Participating restaurants and conditions change frequently; the AGA Web site has the latest information. ⊠ *Rooi Santo 21, Noord* ☎ *297/586–1266, 914/595–4788 in U.S.* ⊕ *www.arubadining.com.*

PRICES AND DRESS

Aruba's elegant restaurants—where you might have to dress up a little (jackets for men, sundresses for women)—can be pricey. If you want to spend fewer florins, opt for the more casual spots, where being comfortable is the only

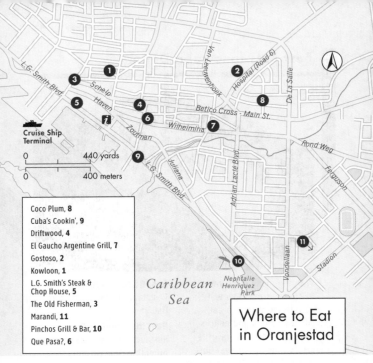

Coco Plum, **8**

Cuba's Cookin', **9**

Driftwood, **4**

El Gaucho Argentine Grill, **7**

Gostoso, **2**

Kowloon, **1**

L.G. Smith's Steak &
Chop House, **5**

The Old Fisherman, **3**

Marandi, **11**

Pinchos Grill & Bar, **10**

Que Pasa?, **6**

Caribbean
Sea

*Nephtalie
Henriquez
Park*

Where to Eat
in Oranjestad

dress requirement. A sweater draped over your shoulders
will go a long way against the chill of air-conditioning. If
you plan to eat in the open air, bring along insect repellent
in case the mosquitoes get unruly.

RESERVATIONS

To ensure that you get to eat at the restaurants of your
choice, make some calls when you get to the island—especially during high season—to secure reservations. Note that
on Sunday you may have a hard time finding a restaurant
that's open for lunch, and that many eateries are closed for
dinner Sunday or Monday.

TIPPING

Most restaurants add a service charge of 15%. It's not necessary to tip once a service charge has been added to the bill,
but if the service is exceptional an additional tip of 10%
is always appreciated. If no service charge is included on
the final bill, then leave the customary tip of 15% to 20%.

Yo, Ho, Ho, and a Cake of Rum

When Venancio Felipe Bareno came to Aruba from Spain more than half a century ago, he probably didn't think that his family's rum cake recipe would make culinary history. Now the sweet little dessert is known around the world. His nephew, Bright Bakery–owner Franklin Bareno, packages the pastry for local and international sales. The history of this island favorite is printed on the side of the box. Made with Aruban Palmeira rum, Natural Bridge Aruba's rum cake makes the perfect gift for folks back home. Available in two sizes, the vacuum-sealed cakes stay fresh for up to six months. The company is registered in the United States, so you can transport the cakes through customs.

ORANJESTAD AND ENVIRONS

$$$$ ✕ **2 Fools and a Bull.** *International.* Friends Paul and Fred have teamed up to offer an evening of culinary entertainment that's more like a fun dinner party than a mere dining experience. Guests are assembled and introduced to one another. Then the evening's meal is explained before everyone sits down at the U-shaped communal dinner table for a five-course culinary adventure. The menu changes daily and there's a selection of suggested wine pairings available by the glass. This isn't a cheap eating-out experience, but it'll certainly be a cherished memory of Aruba. This is one of the few restaurants on the island where reservations are advisable at least a few weeks in advance. ■ TIP➔ Be sure to state any dietary restrictions in advance. ⑤ *Average main: $88* ⊠ *Palm Beach 17, Noord* ☎ *297/586–7177* ⊕ *www.2foolsandabull. com* ⚹ *Reservations essential* ⊙ *Closed Sat. & Sun.*

$ ✕ **Coco Plum.** *Caribbean.* Grab a *pastechi* (meat-, cheese-, or seafood-filled turnover) to go, or stick around to relax under the thatch-roof huts and watch life unfold along Caya Betico Croes. Locals meet here for ham or tuna sandwiches, red-snapper platters, and chicken wings. Slake your thirst with an all-natural fruit drink in flavors such as watermelon, lemon, papaya, tamarind, and passion fruit. At the counter, order *loempias* (egg rolls stuffed with vegetables, chicken, or shrimp) or *empanas* (stuffed pockets of cornmeal). ⑤ *Average main: $11* ⊠ *Caya Betico Croes 100, Oranjestad* ☎ *297/583–1176* ⊟ *No credit cards* ⊙ *Closed Sun. No dinner.*

On Aruba there's no shortage of restaurants serving inventive, fresh-caught seafood dishes.

$$$ ✕ **Cuba's Cookin'.** *Cuban.* Nightly entertainment, great authentic Cuban food, and a lively crowd are the draws here. The empanadas are excellent, as is the chicken stuffed with plantains. Don't leave without trying the roast pork, which is pretty close to perfection. The signature dish is the *ropa vieja*, a sautéed flank steak served with a rich sauce (the name literally translates as "old clothes"). Service can be a bit spotty at times, depending on how busy it gets. There's often live music and dancing is encouraged. ⑤ *Average main: $28* ⊠ *Renaissance Marketplace, L.G. Smith Blvd. 82, Oranjestad* ☎ *297/588–0627* ⊕ *www. cubascookin.com.*

$$$$ ✕ **Driftwood.** *Caribbean.* Charming owner Francine Merry-weather greets you at the door of this Aruban institution, which resembles a series of fishermen's huts. Her husband Herby sets out in his boat every morning, as he has since the late 1980s, to bring the freshest ingredients back to the kitchen. Order his catch prepared as you like (Aruban style—panfried with a fresh tomato, vegetable, and local herbs—is best) or another of the fine fish dishes. The fish soup is based on a family recipe and has been a staple on the menu for more than 25 years. You can't go wrong with the white sangria punch; the maître d' may even let you take home the recipe. This restaurant participates in AGA's Dine-Around program. ⑤ *Average main: $31* ⊠ *Klipstraat*

Aruba's Spicy Cuisine

Arubans like their food spicy, and that's where the island's famous Madame Janette sauce comes in handy. It's made with Scotch bonnet peppers (similar to habanero peppers), which are so hot they can burn your skin when they're broken open. Whether they're turned into *pika*, a relishlike mixture made with papaya, or sliced thin into vinegar and onions, these peppers are sure to set your mouth ablaze. Throw even a modest amount of Madame Janette

sauce into a huge pot of soup and your taste buds will tingle. (Referring to the sauce's spicy nature, Aruban men often refer to an attractive woman as a "Madame Janette.")

To tame the flames, don't go for a glass of water, as capsaicin, the compound in peppers that produces the heat, isn't water soluble. Dairy products (especially), sweet fruits, and starchy foods such as rice and bread are the best remedies.

4

12, Oranjestad ☎ *297/583–2515* ⊕ *www.driftwoodaruba. com* ⊗ *Closed Tues.*

$$$$ ✕ **El Gaucho Argentine Grill.** *Steakhouse.* Faux-leather-bound
FAMILY   books, tulip-top lamps, wooden chairs, and tile floors decorate this Argentina-style steak house, which has been in business since 1977. The key here is meat served in mammoth portions (think 16-ounce steaks) with a range of sides. A welcome feature is a children's playroom, which allows adults to dine while the kids are entertained with videos and games. Be warned, though: even with the kids out of sight, the noise level can still be a bit high in this busy restaurant. ⑤ *Average main: $37* ⊠ *Wilhelminastraat 80, Oranjestad* ☎ *297/582–3677* ⊕ *www.elgaucho-aruba. com* ⊗ *No lunch Sun.*

★   **Fodor's**Choice ✕ **Gostoso.** *Caribbean.* Locals adore the magical
$$$ mixture of Portuguese, Aruban, and international dishes on offer at this consistently excellent establishment. The decor walks a fine line between kitschy and cozy, but the atmosphere is relaxed and informal and outdoor seating is available. The *bacalhau* vinaigrette (dressed salted cod) is a delightful Portuguese appetizer that pairs nicely with most of the Aruban dishes on the menu. Meat lovers are sure to enjoy the Venezuelan mixed grill, which includes a 14-ounce steak and chorizo accompanied by local sides like fried plantain. Service is very attentive and a table visit from the owner is par for the course. ⑤ *Average main: $26* ⊠ *Caya Ing Roland H. Lacle 12, Oranjestad* ☎ *297/588–*

0053 ⊕ *www.gostosoaruba.com* ⚑ *Reservations essential*
☺ *Closed Mon.*

$$$ ✕**Kowloon.** *Asian.* Don't be put off by the dull exterior or off-the-beaten-track location of this fine Asian establishment. The interior decor is tasteful and relaxing, and the combination of Indonesian and authentic Chinese is truly inspired. The most interesting items are in the Epicurean Tour of China section of the menu. The Setju Hoi Sin (the house specialty), a combination of seafood, green pepper, and black beans, is fiery but satisfying. Ⓢ *Average main: $23* ✉ *Emmastraat 11, Oranjestad* ☎ *297/582–4950* ⊕ *www.kowloonaruba.com.*

$$$$ ✕**L.G. Smith's Steak & Chop House.** *Steakhouse.* A study in teak, cream, and black, this fine steak house offers some of the best beef on the island. Subdued lighting and cascading water create a pleasant atmosphere, and the view over L.G. Smith Boulevard to the harbor makes for an exceptional dining experience. The menu features high-quality cuts of meat, all superbly prepared. The casino is steps away if you fancy some slots after dinner. Ⓢ *Average main: $37* ✉ *Renaissance Aruba Beach Resort & Casino, L.G. Smith Blvd. 82, Oranjestad* ☎ *297/523–6195* ⊕ *www.lgsmiths.com* ☺ *No lunch.*

★ **Fodor's**Choice ✕**Marandi.** *Eclectic.* This seaside restaurant,
$$$ whose name means "on the water" in Malaysian, is simultaneously cozy and chic. Tables are tucked under a giant thatched roof by the water's edge. The emphasis here is on Caribbean-influenced dishes using only fresh fish. Popular options include mushroom risotto and the fresh catch of the day. There's a good selection of wines on offer and the waiter will happily suggest the perfect pairing for every course. This is a popular place for romantic occasions and deservedly so. If possible book an early dinner and have cocktails while watching the sun go down with the neighborhood fish swimming about right next to your table. The location is a bit out of the way but worth it for the view and excellent food. Mosquitos can be a problem depending on the time of year, so bring repellent with you or ask the server. Ⓢ *Average main: $27* ✉ *Bucutiweg 50, Oranjestad* ☎ *297/582–0157* ⊕ *www.marandi-aruba.com* ⚑ *Reservations essential* ☺ *No lunch.*

$$$ ✕**The Old Fisherman.** *Seafood.* Although it's not the fanciest place, this downtown institution is popular with locals and is always a good bet for excellent seafood. The catch of the day never disappoints, and neither does the grilled conch, if it's available. The more ambitious can try the 2.2 pounds of fried shrimp. Meat dishes here are not as consistent as the seafood. The sides are basic but filling, and almost every

You can dine directly on the sand at Flying Fishbone in Savaneta.

main course comes with fries, rice, and coleslaw. $ *Average main: $21* ⊠ *Havenstraat 36, Oranjestad* ☎ *297/588–3648.*

★ Fodor'sChoice × **Pinchos Grill & Bar.** *Eclectic.* Built on a pier, this
$$$ casual spot with only 16 tables has one of the most romantic settings on the island. At night the restaurant glimmers from a distance as hundreds of lights reflect off the water. The restaurant's name comes from the Spanish word for a skewered snack, so there are always a few of those on the menu. Guests can watch as chef Erwin Loopstock prepares delectable meals on the grill in his tiny kitchen while owner, Anabela, keeps diners comfortable and happy. The fish-cakes appetizer with a pineapple-mayonnaise dressing is a marriage made in heaven. The bar area is great for enjoying ocean breezes over an evening cocktail, and there is live entertainment every weekend. Many visitors consider a visit to Pinchos an essential part of the Aruba experience. $ *Average main: $24* ⊠ *L.G. Smith Blvd. 7, Oranjestad* ☎ *297/583–2666* ⊘ *No lunch.*

$$$ × **Qué Pasa?.** *Eclectic.* This funky eatery serves as something of an art gallery–restaurant where diners can appreciate the colorful, eclectic works of local artists while enjoying a meal or savoring a drink. The terra-cotta outdoor spaces are illuminated by strings of lights. Inside, jewel-color walls serve as an eye-popping backdrop for numerous paintings. Despite the name, there isn't a Mexican dish on the menu, which includes sashimi, rack of lamb, and fish dishes (they are especially good). Everything is done with Aruban flair,

and the staff is helpful and friendly. Save room for one of the delightfully comforting desserts, such as a brownie with ice cream. The bar area is fun, too. $ *Average main: $22* ⊠ *Wilhelminastraat 18, Oranjestad* ☎ *297/583–4888* ⊕ *www.quepasaaruba.com* ⊗ *No lunch.*

MANCHEBO AND DRUIF BEACHES

$ ╳ **DeliFrance.** *Deli.* If there's a breakfast haven in Aruba, this is it. Skip the usual hotel routine, and head over to this popular deli for a selection of freshly baked bagels and egg dishes galore. DeliFrance is also an excellent choice for lunch, when you can choose from dozens of sandwiches— fillings ranging from the comforting (ham and cheese) to the downright unusual (steak tartare). Save room for one of the hearty desserts, such as sugar waffles with whipped cream and strawberries or a French apple turnover. For java lovers, the coffee alone may be worth the trip. Takeaway sandwiches are a great idea for a hotel room snack later in the day. $ *Average main: $11* ⊠ *Certified Mega Mall, L.G. Smith Blvd. 150, Druif Beach* ☎ *297/588–6006* ⊕ *www. delifrance-aruba.com* ⊗ *No dinner.*

$$$ ╳ **French Steakhouse.** *Steakhouse.* You can hear someone say "ooh-la-la" whenever a sizzling steak is served here. People come from all over the island, which means the lines are often out the door. Classical music plays in the background as the friendly staff serves hearty meat entrées, fresh tuna or grouper, and some vegetarian dishes. A five-course prix-fixe option is available seven nights a week. This eatery participates in AGA's Dine-Around program. $ *Average main: $25* ⊠ *Manchebo Beach Resort, J.E. Irausquin Blvd. 55, Manchebo Beach* ☎ *297/582–3444* ⊕ *www.manchebo. com/steakhouse* ⊗ *No lunch.*

$$ ╳ **The Kitchen.** *Brazilian.* It may take a little work to find this place located just a short drive from the Divi resorts, but your wallet and taste buds will probably thank you for the effort. Though billed as Brazilian cuisine the menu reflects a cosmopolitan approach, and there's something for any taste. The wood-fired grill is a real draw here as is the fact that many of the seafood items on the dinner menu are under $20. Lunch is sold by weight with a choice ranging from sushi to pasta. $ *Average main: $18* ⊠ *150 L.G. Smith Blvd., Druif Beach* ☎ *297/582–3004* ⊗ *Closed Sun.*

$$$$ ╳ **Windows on Aruba.** *International.* Sunset views over the greens to the ocean beyond, live music, and impeccable service make this restaurant in the clubhouse of the Divi

golf course one of the most romantic spots on the island. Menu items include the usual seafood and meat assortment but are exquisitely prepared and beautifully presented. The cauliflower and truffle soup—an excellent starter—reveals an understanding of turning simple ingredients into a complex taste experience. This is one of the better choices for a special evening out on the island. ⑤ *Average main: $35* ⊠ *Divi Village Golf Resort, J.E. Irausquin Blvd. 41, Druif Beach* ☎ *297/730–5017* ⊕ *www.windowsonaruba. com* ⟳ *Reservations essential* ⊘ *No lunch Sat. and Sun.*

EAGLE BEACH

$$$ ╳**Mangos.** *International.* Hotel restaurants are often stuffy, but this is not the case at Mangos. There are no walls here to obscure the view of Eagle Beach, and the food is lovingly prepared, with little fussiness. The creative world menu and relaxed atmosphere attract people from around the island, and Tuesday night features the popular Caribbean buffet, complete with a live folkloric dance show. ⑤ *Average main: $24* ⊠ *Amsterdam Manor, J.E. Irausquin Blvd. 252, Eagle Beach* ☎ *297/587–1492.*

★ **Fodor's** Choice ╳ **Passions on the Beach.** *Caribbean.* Every night
$$$$ the Amsterdam Manor Beach Resort *(⇨ Where to Stay)* transforms the area of Eagle Beach in front of the hotel into a magical and romantic beach dining room. Tiki torches illuminate the white sand, and the linen-covered tables are within inches of the lapping water. Dine on imaginative dishes that are as beautiful as they are delicious. The huge tropical watermelon salad presented in a watermelon half is refreshing and whets the appetite with a slight chili heat. In this "reef cuisine," the main courses lean toward seafood, though meat lovers also are indulged. After dinner, relax with your toes in the sand and enjoy the best show that nature has to offer over signature cocktails. ⑤ *Average main: $30* ⊠ *J.E. Irausquin Blvd. 252, Eagle Beach, Eagle Beach* ☎ *297/527–1100* ⊕ *www.passions-restaurant-aruba. com* ⟳ *Reservations essential.*

$$$ ╳**Screaming Eagle.** *French.* Fine dining in bed is one of the options available at this artistic eatery. The giant "sails" at the entrance and the gentle lighting and billowing white draperies of the interior lend a sophisticated but laid-back air. Menu items are decidedly French in influence but are sometimes deconstructed and always like mini works of art. For an indulgent experience ask for one of the canopy beds and lounge like an emperor while dining. The Dover sole is prepared at the table *à la meunière* (lightly floured and sautéed) and makes for a great photo-op. There's also a three-course chef's menu on offer. ⑤ *Average main: $28* ✉ *J.E. Irausquin Blvd. 228, Eagle Beach* ☎ *297/587–8021* ⊕ *www.screaming-eagle.net* ⊘ *No lunch.*

$$ ✕ **Tulip.** *International.* Despite the decidedly Dutch name the cosmopolitan menu here offers Indonesian, Arabic, French, and numerous other possibilities. Don't let the location at the budget MVC Eagle Beach hotel be a deterrent, as the quality is top-notch and the service is friendly and relaxed. The island's ubiquitous catch of the day is on offer here and is excellent (almost always grouper), or try the chicken satay or the heavy and delicious Aruban dish, *keshi yena* (stuffed cheese). ⑤ *Average main: $17* ✉ *J.E. Irausquin Blvd. 240, Eagle Beach* ☎ *297/587–0110* ⊕ *www. tulip-restaurant-aruba.com.*

PALM BEACH AND NOORD

$$$$ ✕ **Amazonia Churrascaria.** *Steakhouse.* Bring a hearty appetite to this prix-fixe eatery. The emphasis is on meat, but the sweeping salad bar (separately priced) is also available. Bare brick walls, floral displays, and colorful paintings make for a friendly, stylish dining experience. Amazonia participates in AGA's Dine-Around program. ⑤ *Average main: $45* ✉ *J.E. Irausquin Blvd. 374, Palm Beach* ☎ *297/586–4444* ⊕ *www.amazonia-aruba.com* ⊘ *No lunch.*

$$$ ✕ **Amuse Bistro.** *Brasserie.* A bow to French cuisine, Aruban flair, and un-stuffiness is what this popular establishment offers. Diners can choose to sit outside under the stars or in the lively interior, which avoids over-the-top decorating flourishes and lets the menu speak for itself. The menu offers such traditional French items as escargots, and there are Italian and international choices as well. One benefit of dining here is that most menu items are offered in both appetizer and main-course sizes. ⑤ *Average main: $21* ✉ *J.E. Irausquin Blvd. 87, Palm Beach* ☎ *297/596–9949.*

$$$$ ✕ **Aqua Grill.** *Seafood.* Aficionados flock here to enjoy a wide selection of seafood and the largest raw bar on the island. The atmosphere is casual, with a distinctly New England feel. Things can get a little noisy in the open dining room, especially when kids are underfoot (which is often), but a few sips of wine from the extensive list should help numb the effect. Maine lobster and Alaskan king crab legs are available, but why try the usual fare when you can order the Fisherman's Pot, which is filled with scallops, monkfish,

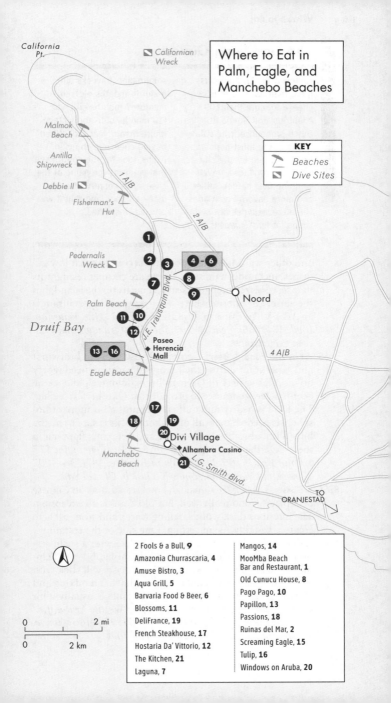

Where to Eat in Palm, Eagle, and Manchebo Beaches

KEY

⊻ Beaches
◲ Dive Sites

California Pt.

◲ Californian Wreck

Malmok Beach

◲ Antilla Shipwreck

◲ Debbie II

Fisherman's Hut

1 A/B

2 A/B

①

②

③

◲ Pedernalis Wreck

④–⑥

⑧

⑨ ○ Noord

⑦

Palm Beach

⑪ ⑩

Druif Bay

⑫

♦ Paseo Herencia Mall

⑬–⑯

4 A/B

Eagle Beach

⑰

⑱

⑲

⑳ Divi Village

♦ Alhambra Casino

Manchebo Beach

㉑

L.G. Smith Blvd.

J.E. Irausquin Blvd.

TO ORANJESTAD

0 ——— 2 mi
0 ——— 2 km

2 Fools & a Bull, **9**
Amazonia Churrascaria, **4**
Amuse Bistro, **3**
Aqua Grill, **5**
Barvaria Food & Beer, **6**
Blossoms, **11**
DeliFrance, **19**
French Steakhouse, **17**
Hostaria Da' Vittorio, **12**
The Kitchen, **21**
Laguna, **7**

Mangos, **14**
MooMba Beach Bar and Restaurant, **1**
Old Cunucu House, **8**
Pago Pago, **10**
Papillon, **13**
Passions, **18**
Ruinas del Mar, **2**
Screaming Eagle, **15**
Tulip, **16**
Windows on Aruba, **20**

CLOSE UP

The Goods on Gouda

Each year Holland exports more than 250,000 tons of cheese to more than 100 countries, and Gouda (the Dutch pronounce it *how*-da) is one of the most popular. Gouda, named for the city where it's produced, travels well and gets harder, saltier, and more flavorful as it ages. There are six types of Gouda: young (at least 4 weeks old), semi-major (8 weeks old), major (4 months old), ultr-amajor (7 months old), old (10 months old), and vintage (more than a year old). When buying cheese in shops in Aruba, look for the control seal that confirms the name of the cheese, its country of origin, its fat content, and that it was officially inspected.

and other seafood? The wood grill serves up great low-cal dishes, including mahimahi. There are cheaper restaurants that serve better-prepared seafood meals on the island, but the variety of offerings here sets it apart. The restaurant is an AGA VIP member. ⑤ *Average main: $41* ⊠ *J.E. Irausquin Blvd. 374, Palm Beach* ☎ *297/586–5900* ⊕ *www.aqua-grill. com* ⊘ *No lunch.*

$$ ✕ **Bavaria Food & Beer.** *German.* Those craving bratwurst and sauerkraut during their tropical vacation need worry no more. A variety of German beers, schnitzel, and a true beer-hall feel guarantee to provide that Oktoberfest feeling. The food is hearty and authentic, but if a bit more atmosphere is needed, the wall of cuckoo clocks is sure to fill the bill. With a bright blue exterior and pennants flapping in the breeze the place is hard to miss. ⑤ *Average main: $17* ⊠ *Palm Beach 186, Noord, Palm Beach* ☎ *297/736–4007* ⊕ *www.bavaria-aruba.com* ⊘ *No lunch. Closed Sun.*

$$$$ ✕ **Blossoms.** *Asian.* Few Aruban hotel restaurants do Chinese or Japanese food really well, but Blossoms is an exception. The interior's dark woods, falling water, and stone all help create a suitably Asian setting. One side of the restaurant is devoted to Japanese cuisine, complete with a sushi station. The expansive menu is a bit daunting, but the helpful staff can ably assist your choice. Purists will stick with one cuisine or the other, but regulars have fun mixing and matching. The hibachi done at your table is usually a hit with kids. ⑤ *Average main: $40* ⊠ *The Westin Aruba, J.E. Irausquin Blvd. 77, Palm Beach* ☎ *297/596–4466* ⊕ *www. westinaruba.com* ⌃ *Reservations essential.*

$$ ✕**Buccaneer.** *Eclectic.* Imagine you're in a sunken ship where
FAMILY sharks, barracudas, and grouper swim past the (rectangular)
portholes. That's what you can find at Buccaneer, a res-
taurant dominated by a 12,000-gallon saltwater aquarium
and where each table has its own individual aquarium. The
chefs prepare passable but not especially noteworthy fare.
The catch of the day is usually a safe bet. The interior and
exterior theme park feel and kitsch make this place great
for those with kids but may prove to be a bit too much for
those without. The restaurant participates in AGA's Dine-
Around program. ⑤ *Average main: $25* ⊠ *Gasparito 11
C, Noord* ☎ *297/586–6172* ⊕ *www.buccaneeraruba.com*
⊘ *Closed Sun. No lunch.*

★ **Fodor's**Choice ✕**Gasparito Restaurant & Art Gallery.** *Caribbean.*
$$$ You can find this enchanting hideaway in a *cunucu* (country)
house in Noord, not far from the hotels. Dine indoors, where
works by local artists are showcased on softly lighted walls, or
on the outdoor patio. Either way, the service is excellent. The
Aruban specialties—pan bati, keshi yena—are feasts for the
eye as well as the palate. The standout dish is the Gasparito
chicken; the sauce recipe was passed down from the owner's
ancestors and features seven special ingredients, including
brandy, white wine, and pineapple juice. (The rest, they say,
are secret.) Gasparito is an AGA Dine-Around member.
⑤ *Average main: $25* ⊠ *Gasparito 3, Noord* ☎ *297/586–7044*
⊕ *www.gasparito.com* ⊘ *Closed Sun. No lunch.*

$$$ ✕**Hostaria Da' Vittorio.** *Italian.* Part of the fun at this family-
oriented spot is watching chef Vittorio Muscariello prepare
authentic Italian regional specialties in the open kitchen.
The staff helps you choose wines from the extensive list
and recommends portions of hot and cold antipasti, risot-
tos, and pastas. Those on a tight budget should stick to
the pizza offerings. Service can be a bit dismissive during
busy periods. As you leave, pick up some limoncello (lemon
liqueur) or olive oil at the gourmet shop. Be aware that the
decibel level of the crowd can be high. A 15% gratuity is
automatically added to your bill. It's an AGA VIP member.
⑤ *Average main: $28* ⊠ *L.G. Smith Blvd. 380, Palm Beach*
☎ *297/586–3838* ⊕ *hostariavittorio.com.*

$$$ ✕**Laguna.** *Caribbean.* Louvered plantation-style doors frame
the view at this colorful Radisson restaurant. You can
dine inside in air-cooled comfort or outside on the terrace
overlooking the lagoon. From Monday through Saturday
a different themed buffet is on offer each night with an
emphasis on seafood. While the quality of the buffet food
is unlikely to win any culinary awards, it is popular (an

Where to Eat Elsewhere on Aruba

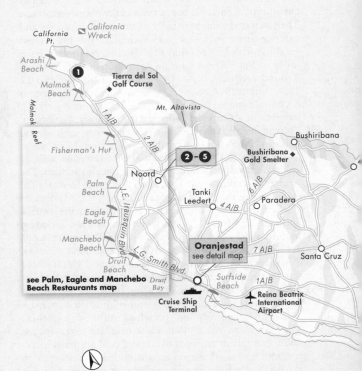

California Pt.

California Wreck

Arashi Beach

Malmok Beach

Malmok Reef

1

Tierra del Sol Golf Course

Mt. Altovista

1 A/B

2 A/B

Fisherman's Hut

Noord

2 - 5

Bushiribana

Bushiribana Gold Smelter

Palm Beach

Tanki Leedert

6 A/B

Paradera

Eagle Beach

4 A/B

J.E. Irausquin Blvd.

Manchebo Beach

Druif Beach

L.G. Smith Blvd.

Oranjestad see detail map

7 A/B

Santa Cruz

see Palm, Eagle and Manchebo Beach Restaurants map

Druif Bay

Surfside Beach

1A/B

Cruise Ship Terminal

Reina Beatrix International Airport

Buccaneer, **2**

Charlie's Restaurant & Bar, **8**

Flying Fishbone, **7**

Gasparito Restaurant & Art Gallery, **3**

Madame Janette's, **4**

The Old Man & The Sea, **6**

Papiamento, **5**

Ventanas del Mar, **1**

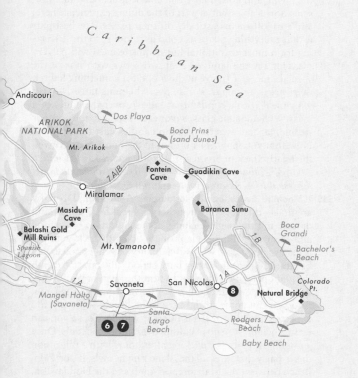

0 4 mi

0 6 km

C a r i b b e a n   S e a

Andicouri

*ARIKOK
NATIONAL PARK*

Dos Playa

Boca Prins
(sand dunes)

Mt. Arikok

7 A/B

Fontein
Cave

Guadikin Cave

Miralamar

Baranca Sunu

Masiduri
Cave

Boca
Grandi

Balashi Gold
Mill Ruins

Bachelor's
Beach

Spanish
Lagoon

Mt. Yamanota

1 B

Savaneta

San Nicolas

1 A

Colorado
Pt.

8

Natural Bridge

Mangel Halto
(Savaneta)

1 A

Santa
Largo
Beach

6 7

Rodgers
Beach

Baby Beach

KEY
⛱ *Beaches*

à la carte menu is also available). The service can be a bit erratic during dinner, but the breakfast buffet is good and reasonably priced. ⑤ *Average main: $30* ⊠ *Radisson Aruba Resort & Casino, J.E. Irausquin Blvd. 81, Palm Beach* ☏ *297/586–6555* ⊕ *www.lagunaaruba.com* ⊗ *No lunch.*

★ **Fodor's**Choice ✕**Madame Janette's.** *European.* Named after
$$$ a local chili pepper (and not a local temptress), this restaurant seems haunted by the spirit of Auguste Escoffier. Large portions and cream sauces are well represented on the menu, and hollandaise and cheese sauces abound. Presentation is an essential part of the dining experience here, and entrées rise majestically off their plates. The best part is that everything tastes as good as it looks, so those looking for a more traditional but exquisite meal will be very pleased. Try the lamb or beef rotisseries with one of the special sauces; if you're in the mood for something lighter, there are tasty salads. For an overwhelming finish, top off your meal with a sundae that billows over the edges of a massive champagne glass. Savor each course in the outdoor pebble garden, where tabletop candles cast a soft glow. Note that you may feel a bit hot in the outdoor area given the relative lack of breezes. ⑤ *Average main: $33* ⊠ *Cunucu Abao 37, Cunucu Abao* ☏ *297/587–0184* ⊕ *www.madame-janette.info* ⟡ *Reservations essential* ⊗ *No lunch.*

$$$ ✕**MooMba Beach Bar & Restaurant.** *American.* Drop by anytime—this festive eatery serves breakfast, lunch, and dinner, and the menu includes a wide selection of seafood and meat specialties. It is probably best to stick with the grilled seafood courses, as the quality of other choices can be erratic, especially during busy periods. By day, sit beneath the giant palapa if you want to beat the heat, or plant yourself at a table in the sand if you haven't had enough sun. And you can come straight from the beach—bare feet are expected here. MooMba is popular with locals, so you can learn a bit about Aruban culture over sunset cocktails. Once a month the place is rollicking after hours with a full-moon dance party that lures all the island's night owls. It's on Palm Beach between the Marriott Surf Club and the Holiday Inn. The restaurant participates in AGA's Dine-Around program. ⑤ *Average main: $25* ⊠ *J.E. Irausquin Blvd. 230, Palm Beach* ☏ *297/586–5365* ⊕ *www.moombabeach.com.*

$$$ ✕**Old Cunucu House.** *Caribbean.* Since the mid-1990s executive chef Ligia Maria has delighted diners with delicious homemade meals, securing her reputation as one of Aruba's finest chefs. Try the *keshi yena* (a meat- and cheese-heavy casserole) or the broiled Caribbean lobster tail, served

CLOSE UP

Chowing Down Aruban Style

With its pristine white-sand beaches, clear blue waters, and near perfect year-round weather, Aruba is a mecca for vacationers looking for a warm getaway. The island as a whole caters to the demanding tourism industry, which has resulted in a mainly resort-food dining scene. But if you're interested in tasting something other than standard American fare—and something a bit more unique to the Dutch- and Caribbean-influenced island—then you ought to try one of these local treats.

Balashi: After a day at the beach there's nothing better than sipping a nice, cold Balashi, Aruba's national beer and the only beer brewed on the island. The taste of Balashi is comparable to a Dutch pilsner.

Bitterballen: Crispy bite-size meatballs, which are breaded and then deep-fried, make for the perfect savory snack or appetizer. Dip them in a side of mustard, and wash them down with a cold Balashi.

Bolita di Keshi: These deep-fried cheese balls are as good as they sound. They make for

a tasty, albeit highly caloric, appetizer.

Funchi: This classic Aruban cornmeal side dish is eaten at all times of day, and it is commonly served with soup.

Keshi Yena: A hearty, stick-to-your-ribs traditional Aruban dish of baked cheese (commonly Gouda) stuffed with chicken, spices, and raisins in a rich brown sauce.

Pan Bati: These pancakelike accompaniments are similar to funchi but slightly sweeter. As opposed to funchi, which is only made of cornmeal, pan bati is a combination of cornmeal, sugar, salt, and baking powder. It's commonly eaten as a side with a meat, fish, or soup entrée.

Pastechi: This empanada-like fried pastry, filled with traditional spiced meat or cheese, is served at all times of day. Although it's a favorite appetizer or snack, pastechi is also a popular breakfast item that can be found at most hotel breakfast buffets.

Saté: Marinated chunks of chicken or pork are skewered on a bamboo stick and then grilled and served with spicy peanut sauce.

with thermidor cream sauce and topped with Parmesan cheese. This is also one of the best places to try Aruba's famous goat stew. For dessert, indulge in Spanish coffee with Tia Maria and brandy. Service can be slow, so relax and enjoy the atmosphere. Friday night features live entertainment. ⑤ *Average main: $26* ⊠ *Palm Beach 150, Palm*

Jumbo shrimp are a delicious staple at Madame Janette's.

Beach 🕾 *297/586–1666* ⊕ *www.theoldcunucuhouse.com* ⊘ *Closed Sun. No lunch.*

$$$$ ✕ **Pago Pago.** *Eclectic.* This elegant and understated restaurant at the Westin may not be the most economical place to eat on the island, but it's certainly one of the nicest. Though the restaurant has built its reputation and following on consistently great steaks, the menu also offers a variety of other excellent choices. The crab cakes served with wasabi are a sure bet, and many swear by the roasted duck. Red-meat lovers may test their mettle on the 24-ounce rib eye. ⑤ *Average main: $31* ✉ *Westin Aruba Resort, J.E. Irasquin Blvd. 77, Palm Beach* 🕾 *297/586–4466* ⊕ *www.westinaruba. com* ⌂ *Reservations essential* ⊘ *Closed Wed. No lunch.*

$$$$ ✕ **Papillon.** *French.* Despite being inspired by Henri Charrière's escape from Devil's Island, the food here couldn't be more removed from bread and water. The owners use the famous autobiography and film as a metaphor for a culinary journey to freedom—they transform classic French cuisine with Caribbean flair. There are whimsical prison touches throughout the restaurant and especially in the washrooms. The menu includes classics like beef bourguignonne but isn't afraid to offer more adventurous dishes such as a standout crispy duck breast served with passion fruit and chocolate. Whatever you order, you'll find the presentation is always impeccable. ⑤ *Average main: $35* ✉ *J.E. Irausquin Blvd. 348A, The Village, Palm Beach* 🕾 *297/586–5400* ⊕ *www. papillonaruba.com* ⌂ *Reservations essential.*

$$$$ ×**Papiamento.** *Eclectic.* The Ellis family converted its 175-year-old manor into a bistro with an atmosphere that is elegant, intimate, and always romantic. You can feast in the dining room, which is filled with antiques, or outdoors on the terrace by the pool (sitting on plastic patio chairs covered in fabric). The chefs mix Continental and Caribbean cuisines to produce sumptuous seafood and meat dishes. Those seeking a bit of novelty can order one of the hot stone dishes, which come to the table sizzling. Service is unhurried, so don't come here if you're in a rush. Ⓢ *Average main: $33* ⊠ *Washington 61, Noord* ☎ *297/586–4544* ⊕ *papiamentoaruba.com* ⊛ *Reservations essential* ⊘ *Closed Mon. No lunch.*

$$$$ ×**Ruinas del Mar.** *Caribbean.* Locally cut limestone walls, lush gardens, and falling water make this one of the most stylish restaurants on the island. Try to get a seat near the torch-lit koi pond. The food is good, not exceptional, but the surroundings make this establishment well worth a visit. The Sunday champagne brunch buffet is a wonder and may be the best bet in terms of price. A 15% service charge is added to your check. Ⓢ *Average main: $39* ⊠ *Hyatt Regency Aruba Beach Resort & Casino, J.E. Irausquin Blvd. 85, Palm Beach* ☎ *297/586–1234* ⊘ *No lunch. No dinner Sun.*

WESTERN TIP (CALIFORNIA DUNES)

$$$$ ×**Ventanas del Mar.** *Eclectic.* Floor-to-ceiling windows provide ample views across the lovely Tierra del Sol golf course and beyond to rolling sand dunes and the sea off the island's western tip. Dining on the intimate terrace amid flickering candles inspires romance. Sandwiches, salads, conch fritters, nachos, and quesadillas fill the midday menu; at night the emphasis is on seafood and meat. Crispy whole red snapper in a sweet-and-sour sauce and crab-and-corn chowder are specialties. The restaurant is an Aruba Gastronomic Association VIP member. Ⓢ *Average main: $32* ⊠ *Tierra del Sol Resort, Malmokweg* ☎ *297/586–7800* ⊕ *www.tierradelsol.com/en/restaurants* ⊘ *Closed Sun. Apr.–Nov.*

SAVANETA

★ Fodor's Choice ×**Flying Fishbone.** *Seafood.* This friendly, relaxed
$$$$ beach restaurant is well off the beaten path in Savaneta, so be sure to have a map in the car. You can dine with your toes in the sand or enjoy your meal on the wooden deck. The emphasis here is on fresh seafood—beautifully

presented on colorful beds of vegetables—but there are good choices for landlubbers, too. The shrimp, shiitake, and blue-cheese casserole is a tried-and-true favorite kept on the menu to keep the regulars happy. This place pulls a crowd year-round. ■TIP→ Arrive early for dinner to get a good table nearer the water. ⑤ *Average main: $34* ⊠ *Savaneta 344, Savaneta* ☎ *297/584–2506* ⊕ *www.flyingfishbone.com* ⌖ *Reservations essential.*

$$$$ ⨯ **The Old Man & The Sea.** *Caribbean.* Local music celebrity Jonathan Vieira and his artist mother Osyth Henriquez have created an open-air restaurant so magical that the food seems almost superfluous. The location requires a cab ride (unless you have a rental car), but the beachfront setting, with tables in the sand, is gorgeous. The menu offers both seafood and the usual steak choices, but there is a distinct Caribbean flavor to almost everything. The spicy Caesar salad and seared catch of the day coated in a spicy papaya marinade are popular choices. The quality of the food and the service can be erratic, and the prices are high even by Aruban standards. Still, it is hard to get too impatient with sand between your toes. Insect repellent is a must if it's been raining. ⑤ *Average main: $40* ⊠ *Savaneta 356A, Savaneta* ☎ *297/735–0840* ⊕ *www.theoldmanandthesearestaurant. com* ⊙ *Closed Sun. No lunch.*

SAN NICOLAS

$$$ ⨯ **Charlie's Restaurant & Bar.** *Caribbean.* Charlie's has been a San Nicolas hangout for more than 50 years. The walls and ceiling are overlaid with license plates, hard hats, sombreros, life preservers, baseball pennants, intimate apparel—you name it. The draw here is the nonstop party atmosphere—somewhere between a frat house and a beach bar. Decent but somewhat overpriced specialties include beef tenderloin and steamed shrimp in the shell. Don't leave before sampling Charlie's "honeymoon sauce" (so called because it's really hot). This may not be the ideal family outing, as it is near the town's red-light district. San Nicolas can be a bit sketchy at night, so you may prefer coming here for lunch. ⑤ *Average main: $23* ⊠ *Zeppenfeldstraat 56, San Nicolas* ☎ *297/584–5086* ⊕ *www.charliesbararuba. com* ⊙ *Closed Sun.*

WHERE TO
STAY

"CUIDA NOS TURISTA" ("Take care of our tourists") is the island's motto, and many Arubans are taught the finer points of hospitality as soon as they learn to read and write. With such cordial hosts, it's hard to go wrong no matter where you decide to stay. Accommodations in Aruba run the gamut from large high-rise hotels and resorts to sprawling time-share condo complexes to small, locally owned boutique establishments.

Most hotels are west of Oranjestad, along L.G. Smith and J.E. Irausquin boulevards. Many are self-contained complexes, with restaurants, shops, casinos, watersports centers, health clubs, and car-rental and travel desks. Room service, laundry and dry-cleaning services, in-room safes, minibars or refrigerators, and babysitting are standard at all but the smallest properties. Most places don't include meals in their rates, although the island now has a few all-inclusive resorts. Still, you can shop around for good dining options, as hotel restaurants and clubs are open to all island guests.

Many people prefer to stay in time-shares, returning year after year and making the island a kind of home away from home. Some time-share patrons say they like the spacious, homey accommodations and the opportunity to prepare their own meals. Note that hotel-type amenities such as shampoo, hair dryers, and housekeeping service may not be offered in time-shares; if they are, they often cost extra. Time-shares and hotels typically charge a combined total of 19% taxes and service charges on top of quoted rates, so be sure to ask about taxes before booking to avoid sticker-shock when you check out.

TYPES OF LODGINGS

Almost all the resorts are along the island's southwest coast, along L.G. Smith and J.E. Irausquin boulevards, the larger high-rise properties being farther away from Oranjestad. A few budget places are in Oranjestad itself. Since most of Aruba's beaches are equally fabulous, it's the resort, rather than its location, that's going to be a bigger factor in how you enjoy your vacation.

Large Resorts: These all-encompassing vacation destinations offer myriad dining options, casinos, shops, watersports centers, health clubs, and car-rental desks. The island has only a handful of all-inclusives, though these are gaining in popularity.

CLOSE UP

Best Bets for Lodging

5

Fodor's offers a selective listing of quality lodging experiences, from the island's best boutique hotel to its most luxurious beach resort. Here we've compiled our top recommendations based on the different types of lodging found on the island. The very best properties—in other words, those that provide a particularly remarkable experience—are designated in the listings with the Fodor's Choice logo.

Fodor's Choice: Amsterdam Manor Beach Resort; Aruba Marriott Resort & Stellaris Casino; Bucuti & Tara Beach Resorts; Hyatt Regency Aruba Beach Resort & Casino; MVC Eagle Beach; Radisson Aruba Resort & Casino; Renaissance Aruba Resort & Casino; Westin Aruba Resort & Casino.

Best Budget Stay: Brickell Bay Beach Club; MVC Eagle Beach; Talk of the Town Hotel & Beach Club.

Best Boutique Hotel: Amsterdam Manor Beach Resort; Bucuti & Tara Beach Resorts.

Best High-Rise Resort: Aruba Marriott Resort & Stellaris Casino; Radisson Aruba Resort & Casino; Westin Aruba Resort & Casino.

Best for Honeymooners: Bucuti & Tara Beach Resorts; Hyatt Regency Aruba Beach Resort & Casino; Radisson Aruba Resort & Casino.

Best for Families: Aruba Beach Club; Costa Linda Beach Resort; Holiday Inn Resort Aruba; Hyatt Regency Aruba Beach Resort & Casino; MVC Eagle Beach; Playa Linda Beach Resort; Renaissance Aruba Resort & Casino.

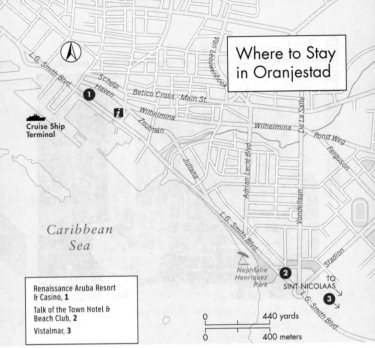

Where to Stay in Oranjestad

Renaissance Aruba Resort & Casino, **1**

Talk of the Town Hotel & Beach Club, **2**

Vistalmar, **3**

Cruise Ship Terminal

Caribbean Sea

Nephtalie Henriquez Park

TO SINT NICOLAAS

| 0 | 440 yards |
| 0 | 400 meters |

Time-shares: Large time-share properties are cropping up in greater numbers, luring visitors who prefer to prepare some of their own meals and have a bit more living space than you might find in the typical resort hotel room.

Boutique Resorts: You'll find a few small resorts that offer more personal service, though not always with the same level of luxury as the larger places. But smaller resorts better reflect the natural sense of Aruban hospitality you'll find all over the island.

PRICES

Hotel rates are high; to save money, take advantage of airline and hotel packages, or visit in summer when rates are discounted by as much as 40%. If you're traveling with kids, ask about discounts; children often stay for free in their parents' room, though there are age cutoffs.

The following reviews have been condensed for this book. For expanded lodging reviews and current deals, visit Fodors.com.

The Renaissance Aruba's private island.

ORANJESTAD AND ENVIRONS

★ **Fodor's**Choice 🖫 **Renaissance Aruba Resort & Casino.** *Resort.* This
$$$ landmark property right on the port offers guests the best of
both worlds—a short walk to the best shopping on the island
and access to a beautiful private beach via a short boat ride
from the hotel lobby. **Pros:** in the heart of the downtown
shopping district; lobby and shopping areas are always
lively; pool area offers an unmatched view of the port; access
to private island with beaches. **Cons:** rooms overlooking
the atrium can be a bit claustrophobic; beach is off-site;
hard to find a quiet spot; no hotel grounds; no balconies in
downtown section. ⑤ *Rooms from: $397* ✉ *L.G. Smith Blvd.
82, Oranjestad* ☎ *297/583–6000, 800/421–8188* ⊕ *www.
renaissancearuba.com* ⌁ *287 rooms, 269 suites* ⊚ *No meals.*

$ 🖫 **Talk of the Town Hotel & Beach Club.** *Hotel.* Bright and airy
rooms (some with kitchenettes) and excellent rates make
this property a great value. **Pros:** great value for money;
close to main shopping area; free breakfast included. **Cons:**
not luxurious; more of a short stay hotel; on one of the
island's busiest street. ⑤ *Rooms from: $229* ✉ *L.G. Smith
Blvd. 2, Oranjestad* ☎ *297/582–3380* ⊕ *www.tottaruba.
com* ⌁ *63 rooms* ⊚ *No meals.*

$ 🖫 **Vistalmar.** *B&B/Inn.* Across the street from the fishing
pier in Oranjestad, Vistalmar is for the budget-minded who
want the comfort of home and don't mind a slightly out-of-
the-way homebase. **Pros:** charming and intimate; very low

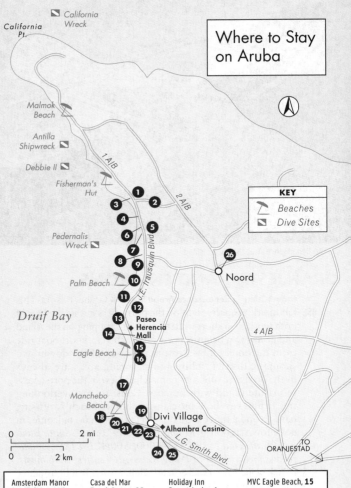

Where to Stay on Aruba

California Pt.

California Wreck

Malmok Beach

Antilla Shipwreck

Debbie II

Fisherman's Hut

1 A/B

2 A/B

Pedernalis Wreck

Palm Beach

J.E. Irausquin Blvd

Druif Bay

Paseo Herencia Mall

Eagle Beach

Manchebo Beach

4 A/B

Noord

26

Divi Village
Alhambra Casino

L.G. Smith Blvd.

TO ORANJESTAD

KEY

Beaches

Dive Sites

1
2
3
4
5
6
7
8
9
10
11
12
13
14
15
16
17
18
19
20
21
22
23
24
25

0   2 mi

0   2 km

Amsterdam Manor Beach Resort, **16**

Aruba Beach Club, **21**

Aruba Divi Phoenix Beach Resort, **13**

Aruba Marriott Resort & Stellaris Casino, **3**

Boardwalk Hotel, **1**

Brickell Bay Beach Club, **5**

Bucuti & Tara Beach Resorts, **18**

Casa del Mar Beach Resort, **22**

Caribbean Palm Village, **26**

Costa Linda Beach Resort, **17**

Divi Aruba Beach Resort All Inclusive, **23**

Divi Dutch Village, **25**

Divi Village Golf & Beach Resort, **19**

Holiday Inn Resort Aruba, **4**

Hotel Riu Palace Aruba, **10**

Hyatt Regency Aruba, **7**

Manchebo Beach Resort & Spa, **20**

Marriott's Aruba Ocean Club, **2**

Mill Resort & Suites, **12**

MVC Eagle Beach, **15**

Occidental Grand Aruba, **8**

Playa Linda Beach Resort, **6**

Radisson Aruba Resort & Casino, **9**

Tamarijn Aruba All-Inclusive Beach Resort, **24**

Tropicana Aruba Resort, **14**

Westin Aruba Resort Casino, **11**

rates allow for up to four adults and kids; homey feeling. **Cons:** not near major shopping area; no beach. ⑤ *Rooms from: $100 ⊠ Bucutiweg 28, Oranjestad* ☎ *297/582–8579* ⊕ *www.arubavistalmar.com* ⌁ *8 rooms* ⊚ *Breakfast.*

MANCHEBO AND DRUIF BEACHES

$ ⌕ **Aruba Beach Club.** *Hotel.* The colonial charm and Dutch
FAMILY hospitality both help keep families coming back year after year. **Pros:** fun, family-friendly atmosphere; great beach; numerous activities; excellent value; lively bars. **Cons:** pool area can be very busy; on-site restaurant is good but a bit pricey; hard to find a quiet spot on the grounds. ⑤ *Rooms from: $200 ⊠ J.E. Irausquin Blvd. 51–53, Punta Brabo Beach* ☎ *297/582–3000* ⊕ *www.arubabeachclub.info* ⌁ *89 rooms, 42 suites* ⊚ *No meals.*

$ ⌕ **Casa del Mar Beach Resort.** *Resort.* Deluxe accommodations
FAMILY at this beachside time-share are quite comfortable, with such amenities as balconies and fully equipped kitchens. **Pros:** home-away-from-home feeling; great beach location; family-friendly. **Cons:** pool area can get crowded; lots of kids; rooms feel a bit dated; few quiet spots on property. ⑤ *Rooms from: $225 ⊠ L.G. Smith Blvd. 53, Punta Brabo Beach* ☎ *297/582–3000, 297/582–7000* ⊕ *www.casadelmararuba.com* ⌁ *147 suites* ⊚ *No meals.*

$$$ ⌕ **Divi Aruba Beach Resort All Inclusive.** *All-Inclusive.* The free
FAMILY food and drinks here and the ability to use the facilities of the adjoining Tamarijn Resort (⇨ *review*) mean you have very little reason to wander far from the idyllic beach location. **Pros:** on wonderful stretch of beach; margarita machines in lobby; common areas feel light and airy; live nightly entertainment. **Cons:** poolside area can get pretty noisy; restaurants are acceptable but not great; rooms could use updating. ⑤ *Rooms from: $667 ⊠ L.G. Smith Blvd. 93, Manchebo Beach* ☎ *297/582–3300, 800/554–2008* ⊕ *www.diviaruba.com* ⌁ *203 rooms* ⊚ *All-inclusive* ⌖ *5-night minimum.*

$ ⌕ **Divi Dutch Village.** *Hotel.* A pair of free-form freshwater pools are at the center of this quiet, oceanfront time-share. **Pros:** beautiful beach is just steps away, and supermarkets are within walking distance; quieter than the other Divi properties on the beach. **Cons:** not directly on the beach; no ocean views from any rooms; close to a busy intersection; rooms could use updating; Wi-Fi can be spotty. ⑤ *Rooms from: $235 ⊠ J.E. Irausquin Blvd. 47, Druif Beach* ☎ *297/583–5000, 800/367–3484* ⊠ *297/582–0501* ⊕ *www. dividutchvillage.com* ⌁ *97 units* ⊚ *No meals.*

5

$$ 🏨 **Divi Village Golf & Beach Resort.** *Resort.* Although it's just across the road from its sister Divi properties, this all-suites version is quieter and more refined. **Pros:** excellent golf course; spacious rooms; lushly landscaped grounds; great savings for being a mere 20 yards from the beach. **Cons:** bit of a hike from some rooms to the lobby; you must cross a busy road to get to the beach; it might be a bit too quiet for some. ⑤ *Rooms from: $245* ✉ *J.E. Irausquin Blvd. 93, Oranjestad* ☎ *297/583–5000, 297/583–5000* ⊕ *www.divivillage.com* 🛏 *250 suites* ⦿ *Multiple meal plans* ⌁ *3-night minimum.*

$$ 🏨 **Manchebo Beach Resort & Spa.** *Resort.* Amid 100 acres of gardens, Manchebo Beach Resort feels miles away from it all; in reality it's five minutes from town and across from a complex with shops, restaurants, and a casino. **Pros:** great beach location; nearby casino; good on-site restaurant; intimate feel. **Cons:** lacks some of the amenities of a larger resort; beach area can get crowded. ⑤ *Rooms from: $310* ✉ *J.E. Irausquin Blvd. 55, Manchebo Beach* ☎ *297/582–3444, 800/223–1108* ⊕ *www.manchebo.com* 🛏 *72 rooms* ⦿ *Multiple meal plans.*

$$$ 🏨 **Tamarijn Aruba All-Inclusive Beach Resort.** *All-Inclusive.* An upscale alternative to its sister property, the Divi Aruba (⇨ *above*), this resort is pleasantly laid-back for an all-inclusive. **Pros:** stunning beach; access to the Divi Aruba All Inclusive next door; perfect for families. **Cons:** being right on the beach can mean noise during busy periods; the linear layout means some rooms are quite far from the lobby; Wi-Fi is an additional charge. ⑤ *Rooms from: $667* ✉ *J.E. Irausquin Blvd. 41, Punta Brabo* ☎ *297/525–5200, 800/554–2008* ⊕ *www.tamarijnaruba.com* 🛏 *236 rooms, 97 suites* ⦿ *All-inclusive* ⌁ *3-night minimum.*

EAGLE BEACH

★ **Fodor's** Choice 🏨 **Amsterdam Manor Beach Resort.** *Hotel.* For an
$$ excellent value check out this intimate, family-run hotel
FAMILY with a genuinely friendly staff and an authentic Dutch-Caribbean atmosphere. **Pros:** feels like a European village; very good family restaurant; friendly and helpful staff; minigrocery on-site; modern and airy rooms; public bus stop in front of hotel for easy access to downtown and the high-rise area. **Cons:** across the road from the beach; lacks the boutiques and attractions of a larger hotel; small pool. ⑤ *Rooms from: $320* ✉ *J.E. Irausquin Blvd. 252, Eagle Beach* ☎ *297/527–1100, 800/932–6509* ⊕ *www.amsterdam-manor.com* 🛏 *68 rooms, 4 suites* ⦿ *No meals.*

The beachfront at Bucuti and Tara Beach Resorts.

★ Fodor's Choice ⚅ **Bucuti & Tara Beach Resorts.** *Resort.* An extraor-
$$$ dinary beach setting, impeccably understated service, and
attention to detail help this elegant Green Globe resort easily
outclass anything else on the island. **Pros:** great atmosphere;
impeccable service; luxurious without insulating guests from
island life; free Wi-Fi throughout; free use of netbooks dur-
ing stay; no kids means a bit more peace and quiet. **Cons:**
beach can get busy, because other hotels share it; little to buy
at hotel; no room service. ⑤ *Rooms from: $451 ⊠ L.G. Smith
Blvd. 55B, Eagle Beach ☎ 297/583–1100 ⊕ www.bucuti.com
➥ 63 rooms, 38 suites, 3 bungalows* ⊙ *Breakfast.*

$$$ ⚅ **Costa Linda Beach Resort.** *Resort.* The aptly named "Beau-
FAMILY tiful Coast" time-share resort is spread along a pristine
600-foot stretch of Eagle Beach. **Pros:** beautiful location;
perfect for families, with many activities available; beautifully landscaped grounds. **Cons:** large resort lacks intimacy;
kids are everywhere; more expensive than some comparable
properties in the area. ⑤ *Rooms from: $378 ⊠ J.E. Irausquin
Blvd. 59, Eagle Beach ☎ 297/583–8000 ⊕ www.costalinda-
aruba.com ➥ 155 suites* ⊙ *No meals.*

★ Fodor's Choice ⚅ **MVC Eagle Beach.** *Hotel.* What started as a
$ vacation facility for the visiting families of Dutch marines
FAMILY is now a great bargain hotel across from Eagle Beach. **Pros:**
unbeatable price; popular restaurant with food at affordable prices; since the main language is Dutch, you feel
that you're someplace other than South Florida here; very
short walk to beach; friendly and helpful staff; attentive

Amsterdam Manor Beach Resort, a small hotel on Eagle Beach, is still family-run.

staff. **Cons:** Spartan accommodations; not for those who want to be away from kids. $\boxed{\text{S}}$ *Rooms from: $150* ✉ *J.E. Irausquin Blvd. 240, Eagle Beach* ☎ *297/587–0110* ⊕ *www. mvceaglebeach.com* ⤳ *16 rooms, 3 suites* ◎ *No meals.*

$ ⊞ **Tropicana Aruba Resort & Casino.** *Resort.* An excellent
FAMILY waterslide, fast-food options, and a nearby supermarket make this complex of self-contained time-share units right across from Eagle Beach a popular choice for families. **Pros:** self-catering can be great for families; Dunkin' Donuts and pizza restaurant on the compound; new supermarket right across the street; price is hard to beat for a hotel so close to the beach. **Cons:** feels like an apartment complex; public areas are noisy and crowded; beach is across a road; despite the attractions for children there are no kids' programs available. $\boxed{\text{S}}$ *Rooms from: $161* ✉ *J.E. Irausquin Blvd. 250, Eagle Beach* ☎ *297/587–9000, 800/835–7193* ⊕ *www.troparuba.com* ⤳ *362 suites* ◎ *No meals.*

PALM BEACH AND NOORD

$$ ⊞ **Aruba Divi Phoenix Beach Resort.** *Resort.* A breathtaking location, a lively atmosphere, and relatively reasonable rates make this hotel justifiably popular. **Pros:** great beach; small grocery store on premises; lively crowd at the beach bar. **Cons:** beach can get crowded during peak times; not near major shopping areas. $\boxed{\text{S}}$ *Rooms from: $349* ✉ *J.E. Irausquin Blvd. 75, Palm Beach* ☎ *297/586–1170* ⊕ *www.*

Associations That Accommodate

Aruba Apartment Resort & Small Hotel Association. This group represents smaller, less expensive hotels. Members are expected to meet certain standards of accommodations and service and still offer affordable rates, which are often as low as $65 per night. ☎ 297/582–3289.

Aruba Hotel & Tourism Association. The Aruba Hotel & Tourism Association was established in 1965 to maintain high standards in the tourism industry. From its original seven hotels, the organization has grown to more than 80 businesses, including restaurants, casinos, stores, tour operators, and airlines. The organization's budget, earmarked to promote Aruba as a travel destination, comes from a 7.5% room tax that funds both it and the newly privatized Aruba Tourism Authority. You can express opinions and register complaints on the Aruba Tourism ebsite, ⊕ www.aruba. com. The organization is also involved in anti-litter efforts as part of the Aruba Limpi Committee. ☎ 297/582–2607 ⊕ www.ahata.com.

diviarubaphoenix.com ➫ 60 rooms, 151 1-bedroom suites, 21 2-bedroom suites, 8 3-bedroom suites ⭐No meals.

★ Fodor'sChoice ⛝ **Aruba Marriott Resort & Stellaris Casino.** *Resort.*
$$$$ The gentle sound of the surf and splashing waterfalls create the backdrop of this sprawling compound, where everything seems to run smoothly. **Pros:** large rooms; variety of excellent restaurants; great shopping; every imaginable service is conveniently on-site. **Cons:** large, impersonal resort; reception can become gridlocked in peak season; ongoing construction of another hotel next door. ⑤ *Rooms from: $569* ⊠ *L.G. Smith Blvd. 101, Palm Beach* ☎ 297/586–9000, 800/223–6388 ⊕ *www.marriott.com* ➫ 388 rooms, 23 suites ⭐No meals.

$ ⛝ **Boardwalk Hotel Aruba.** *Hotel.* Although the Boardwalk Hotel is just a few yards from the beach and within walking distance of casinos, it manages to remain well insulated from the hustle and bustle. **Pros:** right in the middle of activities of the high-rise area; great restaurants within walking distance; close to beach. **Cons:** not right on the beach; no restaurants in compound; limited views. ⑤ *Rooms from: $305* ⊠ *Bakval 20, Palm Beach* ☎ 297/586–6654 ⊕ *www.boardwalkaruba.com* ➫ 11 1-bedroom suites, 2 2-bedroom suites ⭐No meals.

DID YOU KNOW?

Aruba has about 8,000 hotel rooms and time-share accommodations, most of which are lined up along Palm and Eagle beaches on the island's west coast.

The Aruba Marriott Resort & Stellaris Casino is in the heart of Palm Beach.

$ ⛅ **Brickell Bay Beach Club.** *Hotel.* For a hotel that's just a few minutes away from the high-rise hotels and Palm Beach, Brickell Bay has rates that are extremely reasonable. **Pros:** good rates for a location near the luxury resorts; complimentary breakfast; free shuttles to beach and casinos. **Cons:** no direct beach access; lacks amenities of larger properties; uninspiring views; some rooms are in need of renovation. ⓈRooms from: $215 ⊠J.E. Irausquin Blvd. 370, Palm Beach ☎297/586–0900 ⊕www.brickellbayaruba.com ➴94 rooms, 4 suites ⦿No meals.

$ ⛅ **Caribbean Palm Village.** *Hotel.* Some of the one- and two-
FAMILY bedroom accommodations at this tile-roof resort not far from Palm Beach have fully equipped kitchens, and all have private balconies. **Pros:** excellent for families; good security on-site; friendly staff; lively pool area. **Cons:** no beach; some rooms feel dated; laid-back atmosphere might be a bit too quiet for younger adults without children. ⓈRooms from: $188 ⊠Palm Beach Rd., Noord 43E, Noord ☎297/586–2700 ⊕www.cpvr.com ➴170 rooms ⦿No meals.

$ ⛅ **Holiday Inn Resort Aruba.** *Resort.* This popular, family-
FAMILY oriented package-tour resort has three seven-story buildings filled with spacious rooms lining a sugary, palm-dotted shore. **Pros:** affordable; great beachfront location; lots of activities for the kids. **Cons:** hallways feel a little institutional; lines at reception can make you feel you are back at the airport; some rooms in need of refurbishment; restaurants are mediocre at best and service can be a problem.

⑤*Rooms from: $251* ⊠*J.E. Irausquin Blvd. 230, Palm Beach* ☎*297/586–3600, 800/465–4329* ⊕*www.caribbeanhi.com/aruba* ⤳*600 rooms, 7 suites* �ﻬ*No meals.*

$$$$ ☒**Hotel Riu Palace Aruba.** *All-Inclusive.* This white wedding cake of a resort towers over Palm Beach with one eight-story and two 10-story towers. **Pros:** beautiful vistas; drink dispensers in all rooms; large and lively pool area. **Cons:** pool area is always crowded and loud; unimpressive à la carte restaurants; interior decor is a bit out of place for an island destination. ⑤*Rooms from: $520* ⊠*J.E. Irausquin Blvd. 79, Palm Beach* ☎*297/586–3900, 800/345–2782* ⊕*www.riuaruba.com* ⤳*450 rooms* ﻬ*All-inclusive.*

★ Fodor's Choice ☒**Hyatt Regency Aruba Beach Resort & Casino.**
$$$$ *Resort.* This 12-acre property is popular with families,
FAMILY but honeymooners head here, too, because the resort is big enough to provide quiet, romantic corners. **Pros:** beautiful grounds; great for kids; excellent restaurants. **Cons:** small balconies for a luxury hotel; some rooms are quite a stretch from the beach. ⑤*Rooms from: $565* ⊠*J.E. Irausquin Blvd. 85, Palm Beach* ☎*297/586–1234, 800/554–9288* ⊕*www.aruba.hyatt.com* ⤳*342 rooms, 18 suites* ﻬ*No meals.*

$$$$ ☒**Marriott's Aruba Ocean Club.** *Rental.* First-rate amenities
FAMILY and lavishly decorated villas have made this time-share the talk of the island. **Pros:** relaxed atmosphere; feels more like a home than a hotel room; excellent beach. **Cons:** bit of a hike to restaurants at hotel next door; pricey; attracts large families, so kids are everywhere. ⑤*Rooms from: $675* ⊠*L.G. Smith Blvd. 99, Palm Beach* ☎*297/586–2641* ⊕*www.marriott.com* ⤳*93 rooms, 213 suites* ﻬ*No meals.*

$ ☒**Mill Resort & Suites.** *Resort.* A short walk from the beach,
FAMILY this low-rise resort is laid out around a busy pool and bar area, and the open-air Mediterranean-style lobby has free coffee day and night. **Pros:** entire compound has an intimate feel; lively bar area; theme nights are fun; numerous activities to keep kids amused. **Cons:** not on the beach; pool area can be busy and noisy; rates are not the steal they used to be. ⑤*Rooms from: $267* ⊠*J.E. Irausquin Blvd. 330, Palm Beach* ☎*297/586–7700* ⊕*www.millresort.com* ⤳*64 studios, 121 suites* ﻬ*Multiple meal plans.*

$$$$ ☒**Occidental Grand Aruba.** *All-Inclusive.* Popular with tour groups, this all-inclusive resort always has something going on, whether it's beer-drinking contests or bikini fashion shows. **Pros:** gorgeous rooms; great beach location; wide range of activities available. **Cons:** beach and pool can get crowded, and free drinks means noise; as at most all-inclusives, the food is lackluster. ⑤ *Rooms from: $637* ✉ *J.E. Irausquin Blvd. 83, Palm Beach* ☎ *297/586–4500, 800/448–8355* ⊕ *www. occidentalgrandaruba.com* ⇨ *398 rooms* ⦿ *All-inclusive.*

$$ ⚏ **Playa Linda Beach Resort.** *Resort.* On one of the nicest
FAMILY sections of Palm Beach, this striking resort is constructed like a stepped Mayan pyramid. **Pros:** great beach location; tastefully decorated rooms; lots of distractions for the kids. **Cons:** Wi-Fi reception varies depending on room location; not all rooms are of the same standard. ⑤ *Rooms from: $315* ✉ *J.E. Irausquin Blvd. 87, Palm Beach* ☎ *297/586– 1000* 🖷 *297/586–5210* ⊕ *www.playalinda.com* ⇨ *66 studios, 95 1-bedroom suites, 33 2-bedroom suites, 18 town houses* ⦿ *Breakfast.*

★ Fodor'sChoice ⚏ **Radisson Aruba Resort & Casino.** *Resort.* The
$$$$ lavish rooms at this 14-acre resort are appointed with colo-
FAMILY nial West Indian–style furniture, and their large balconies overlook the ocean or tropical gardens. **Pros:** rooms feel homey; top-notch fitness center; one of the best spas on the island; free high-speed Internet in rooms. **Cons:** restaurants are good but not great; some rooms are on the small side and don't seem worth the cost. ⑤ *Rooms from: $601* ✉ *J.E. Irausquin Blvd. 81, Palm Beach* ☎ *297/586–6555* ⊕ *www. radisson.com* ⇨ *321 rooms, 34 suites* ⦿ *No meals.*

★ Fodor'sChoice ⚏ **Westin Aruba Resort & Casino.** *Resort.* Although
$$$$ these tasteful rooms aren't as large as those at nearby resorts,
FAMILY they are beautifully furnished, with plentiful wood accents. **Pros:** chic and airy rooms; magnificent beachfront and pool area; comprehensive spa facilities; great restaurants. **Cons:** immediate area is congested and busy; rooms are not as modern feeling as some nearby resorts; resort feels vast (and it is). ⑤ *Rooms from: $379* ✉ *J.E. Irausquin Blvd. 77, Palm Beach* ☎ *297/586–4466, 877/822–2222* ⊕ *www.westinaruba.com* ⇨ *481 rooms, 81 suites* ⦿ *No meals.*

NIGHTLIFE AND THE ARTS

THEY PUMP UP THE VOLUME at Aruba's resort bars when the sun sets. Unlike many other islands, nightlife here isn't confined to touristy folkloric shows. In addition to spending time in one of the many casinos, you can slowly savor a drink while the sun dips into the sea, dance to the beat of a local band, barhop in a colorful bus, or simply stroll along a deserted starlit beach.

Arubans like to party—the more the merrier—and they usually start celebrating late in the evening. The action, mostly on weekends, doesn't pick up until around midnight. Casual yet trendy attire is the norm. Most bars don't have a cover charge, although most nightclubs do. Bigger clubs, such as Havana Beach Club, may have lines on weekends, but they move quickly; use this time to start your socializing, and you may just end up with a dance partner before you even set foot inside the door. Drink specials are available at some bars, and every establishment will gladly give you a free Balashi Cocktail (the local term for a glass of water). Both bars and clubs have either live bands or DJs, depending on the night.

No matter where you choose to party, be smart about getting back to your hotel. Drinking then driving, of course, is against the law. If you're within walking distance, go ahead and hoof it. Taxis are a good option if your hotel is farther away. The island is safe, and you'll probably wander with swarms of other visitors in town and along Palm Beach.

NIGHTLIFE

For information on specific events, check out the free magazines *Aruba Nights, Aruba Events, Aruba Experience,* and *Aruba Holiday,* all available at the airport and at hotels.

SUNSET CRUISE

Mi Dushi. You can take a Sunset Happy Hour Cruise aboard this 80-foot sailing vessel, where you can enjoy snacks as you toast with champagne. The open-air bar serves drinks made with premium brands (they are included in your ticket price). Cruises depart Wednesday and Friday at 5 pm from the De Pal Pier between the Riu Palace and the Radisson, returning about 7 pm. The cost is $39 per person. ☎ 297/586–2010 ⊕ *www.midushi.com.*

A sunset happy-hour cruise is a popular pastime.

WEEKLY PARTIES

★ Fodor'sChoice **Bon Bini Festival.** This year-round folklore event (the name means "welcome" in Papiamento) is held every Tuesday from 6:30 pm to 8:30 pm at Ft. Zoutman in Oranjestad. In the inner courtyard you can check out the Antillean dancers in resplendent costumes, feel the rhythms of the steel drums, browse among the stands displaying local artwork, and sample local food and drink. Admission is usually around $3, but can be as high as $10, depending on what is on offer. ⊠ *Oranjestad.*

ORANJESTAD AND ENVIRONS

BARS

Iguana Joe's. The reptilian-themed decor is as colorful and creative as the specialty cocktails served here. A favorite hangout for those who want to enjoy the view of the port from the second-floor balcony. The crowd is primarily tourists during the early evening, and many locals enjoy the laid-back vibe on Friday and Saturday nights. ⊠ *Royal Plaza Mall, L.G. Smith Blvd. 94, Oranjestad* ☎ *297/583-9373* ⊕ *www.iguanajoesaruba.com.*

DANCE CLUBS AND MUSIC CLUBS

7 West. A fun atmosphere prevails on Friday when the great view of the harbor, live music, and specialty drinks keep spirits high. On Tuesday night bands from the cruise ships take the stage. ⊠ *Weststraat 7, Oranjestad* ☎ *297/588–9983* ⊕ *www.7-westaruba.com.*

CILO. Live bands perform most weekends at this popular downtown hangout, whose name is short for "City Lounge." The food is great, but most people come for drinks and to enjoy the view and great music. ⊠ *Renaissance Marketplace, L.G. Smith Blvd. 82, Oranjestad* ☎ *297/588–7996* ⊕ *www.CILO-aruba.com.*

Garufa Cigar & Cocktail Lounge. Most nights there's jazz and other live entertainment at this cozy spot, which serves as a lounge for customers waiting for a table at the nearby Gaucho Argentine Grill (you're issued a beeper so you know when your table is ready). While you wait, have a drink, enjoy some appetizers, and take in the leopard-print carpet and funky bar stools. The ambience may very well draw you back for an after-dinner cognac. A powerful smoke-extractor system helps keep the air clear. ⊠ *Wilhelminastraat 63, Oranjestad* ☎ *297/582–7205* ⊕ *www.facebook. com/Garufa.Aruba.*

Nikky Beach. This upscale hot spot is party central on Friday night. Local bands perform on Sunday. The venue is often booked for special events so call ahead. ⊠ *L.G. Smith Blvd. 2, Oranjestad* ☎ *297/582–0153* ⊕ *www.nikky beacharuba.com.*

MANCHEBO AND DRUIF BEACHES

BARS

Pelican Terrace. Sip creative cocktails, dance around the pool, and grab a late-night snack—perhaps a pizza that's piping hot from the wood-burning oven. Live music every evening makes this a popular nightspot. A busy scene is guaranteed, as most of the other patrons are resort guests enjoying all-inclusive drinks. ⊠ *Divi Aruba Beach Resort, J.E. Irausquin Blvd. 45, Druif Beach* ☎ *297/582–3300* ⊕ *www.diviaruba.com/bars-lounges.*

L.G. Smith Boulevard: The Strip of Aruba

CLOSE UP

Whether you arrive by land or sea, the first street you'll encounter is L.G. Smith Boulevard. Many cruise-ship arrivals never bother to explore anywhere else, as there are malls, nightclubs, high-end shopping, and enough "One Happy Island" T-shirt variations to annoy all their friends and relatives back home. This primary artery runs along the marina, and includes some of the island's best shopping and nightspots. The busiest part of the boulevard runs from Renaissance Marketplace to the cruise-ship dock, and is filled with car and pedestrian traffic every day until the very early hours of the morning.

Though Aruba is normally overflowing with visitors, there's keen competition on the strip to attract customers. Like tropical flowers seeking pollination, many of the L.G. Smith bars and restaurants use garish colors to get the attention of passersby. Bars like Mambo Jambo, which has a second-floor location, add loud music to their eye-popping paint job in order to entice potential customers up the steps. On weekends L.G. Smith Boulevard becomes the place for young people to see and be seen. Young men spend much of the evening driving their tricked-out cars up and down the street, often with music blasting from their sound systems. L.G. Smith Boulevard is the vibrant and noisy heart and soul of this nightlife-obsessed island.

6

EAGLE BEACH

BARS/DANCE CLUBS

Pata Pata Bar. The pool deck at La Cabana Resort has a fun swim-up bar where locals and guests go for a festive atmosphere and the two-for-one happy hour daily from 4–6. Musicians take the stage every evening. ⊠ *La Cabana Beach Resort and Casino, J.E. Irausquin Blvd. 250, Eagle Beach* ☎ *297/587–9000* ⊕ *www.lacabanabrc.com/food-beverage.*

PALM BEACH AND NOORD

BARS

Alfresco Bar. Guests gather at Alfresco, the Hyatt's lobby bar, to hear live music early in the evening and for a nightcap after the casino closes. Alfresco offers a view of Hyatt's elaborate swimming pool with whirlpools, waterslides, and waterfalls. ⊠ *Hyatt Regency Aruba Beach Resort & Casino, J.E. Irausquin Blvd. 85, Palm Beach* ☎ *297/586–1234.*

Brewing Up Something Special

There was a time when you could walk into any bar in Aruba and get a glass of water by asking for a Balashi Cocktail. (The name came from the fact that the desalination plant is in an area known as Balashi.) Since the creation of Balashi, the first locally brewed beer, such a drink order has taken on a whole new meaning.

Made by a German brewmaster in a state-of-the-art facility, Balashi is a golden-color pilsner. The beer is a source of local pride, even more so since it won the prestigious Monde Selection at an international competition in 2001. Visitors love it as well. "It's a big tourist thing," explains Gerben Tilma, general manager of the plant. "Everyone wants to know what the best local products are. Now we can tell them."

Balashi Brewery. The Balashi Brewery has free one-hour tours at 10 am weekdays. There's also a souvenir shop, a café, and a 10,000-square-foot beer garden where you can enjoy a cold one. ⊠ *Balashi* ☎ *297/585–4805.*

Bugaloe. Beauties in skimpy bathing suits and windsurfers in baggy shorts come to this beachfront spot for margaritas and sunset and after-dark partying. There's live reggae, salsa, and pop on Friday and Sunday. ⊠ *De Palm Pier, J.E. Irausquin Blvd. 79, De Palm Pier, Palm Beach* ☎ *297/586–2233.*

Café Rembrandt. This Dutch-style café pulls in a loud, fun crowd, especially for the live music on Wednesday and Friday. Dancing tends to erupt spontaneously. The food is cheap and delicious. ⊠ *South Beach Centre, Palm Beach* ☎ *297/586–4747* ⊕ *www.rembrandt-aruba.com.*

MooMba Beach Bar. If you're looking to enjoy a cocktail with your toes in the cool sand, MooMba is your place. Enjoy tropical cocktails under a giant, thatched-roof that shades couches, lounges, and circular bar. ⊠ *Between Holiday Inn and Marriott Surf Club, J.E. Irausquin Blvd. 230, Palm Beach* ☎ *297/586–5365* ⊕ *www.moombabeach.com.*

Palms Beach Bar. Here you'll have front-row seats to view the phenomenon known as the green flash—a ray of green light that sometimes flicks through the sky as the sun sinks into the ocean. Optical events aside, the Palms is the perfect spot to enjoy the sunset with a drink in-hand. ⊠ *Hyatt*

CLOSE UP

Barhopping Buses

Banana Bus. For $45-per-person, you can enjoy a ride in a bus with a 20-foot banana mounted on the roof! But the real fun is that this party bus makes its way to a number of lively, local bars, and five drinks are included in the price. Reservations can be made at your hotel front desk. The bus will pick you up there as well. ⊕ www.bananabusa-ruba.com.

Kukoo Kunuku. To many repeat visitors, this wander-ing party bus is an integral part of the Aruba experience. Every night except Sunday you can find as many as 40 passengers traveling among three bars from sundown to around midnight. The $65 fee per passenger includes a so-so dinner, some drinks, and pickup at your hotel. The main point is the nonstop entertainment and the chance to make friends with a fun-loving crowd. ☎ 297/586–2010 ⊕ www.ku-kookunuku.com.

Regency Aruba Beach Resort & Casino, J.E. Irausquin Blvd. 85, Palm Beach ☎297/586–1234.

Señor Frog's. True to most of its locations, this chain bar is a hot spot that pulls a wild crowd. The music is loud, and the crowd is pumped up by the animated staff and such alcoholic favorites as the yard of beer (you can also buy a yard of margarita). Either way you can take the glass home with you. Definitely a popular stop for younger partiers. ⊠ *J.E. Irausquin Blvd. 348A, Noord, Palm Beach* ☎297/586-8900.

DANCE AND MUSIC CLUBS

Gilligan's. The Radisson's beachside bar puts local bands in the spotlight. The decor and view will make you feel as if you've been shipwrecked on an uncharted tropical isle, albeit one with a fully stocked bar. ⊠ *Radisson Aruba Caribbean Resort, J.E. Irausquin Blvd. 81, Palm Beach* ☎297/586–6555.

THEME PARTIES

At last count there were more than 50 theme nights offered during the course of a week. Each party features a buffet dinner, dancing, and entertainment (often of the limbo, steel-band, stilt-walking variety). For a complete list, contact the Aruba Tourism Authority.

6

DID YOU KNOW?

The Kukoo Kunuku always starts with a champagne toast at the California Light-house followed by dinner and barhopping until midnight. It's one of the most popular nightlife activities in Aruba.

CLOSE UP

In Tune with Jonathan Vieira

His parents were always traveling, so when musician Jonathan Vieira was growing up he often stayed with his grandmother. He was fascinated with her old piano. He hit his first note when he was four, and has been playing ever since. The Aruba native, who taught himself to play, recorded an album called *Two Generations* with Padu del Caribe, one of the composers of the island's national anthem. Vieira speaks highly of his collaborator, calling him the "father of our culture."

"On Aruba, people need to have more of an awareness of cultural music," Vieira says. "The popular stuff catches on quick; we have to have a balance."

Many of his own musical creations show his affinity for local rhythms, though he also is well versed in classical and contemporary music.

When he was about 14, a local promoter heard about his talents and invited him to open one of the concerts she was organizing. The reaction was positive, and for the first time

Vieira realized he could use his talent to make some money—or at least pay his school expenses. At age 17, Vieira headed to the United States to continue his education. He attended the Berkeley College of Business in New York City, where he earned a degree in information management systems. It was his third degree; the others are in film and video production and recording arts production. "On the island," says Vieira, "everyone knows me as a pianist."

Although his first love is music, Vieira has also been dabbling in film. "I have been doing a bit of acting recently to try it out," he says. In the meantime, Vieira is busy giving back to the island he calls home. He's opened a new beach restaurant, The Old Man and The Sea, in collaboration with his mother and he's spending much more time on the island. Vieira gives chamber concerts at the Access, an art gallery and performance space in Oranjestad. He also invites other artists to join him in special holiday performances.

Aruba Marriott Resort & Stellaris Casino. Don't pass up the fun Carnival-themed show here just because it's at a hotel. It happens every Tuesday night outdoors at Waves Beach Bar. Costumed dancers perform to calypso and Latin music to the delight of tourists and locals alike. After a few cocktails even shy audience members seem willing to accept the call to join in for a dance or two. ⊠ *L.G. Smith Blvd. 101, Palm Beach* ☎ *297/586–9000.*

Cool Concoctions

These drink recipes come from Aruban-born bartender Clive Van Der Linde.

■ **The Wow.** Mix equal parts (2 ounces or so) of rum and vodka as well as triple sec, a splash of tequila, grenadine, coconut cream, and pineapple and orange juice. Quips Van Der Linde, "You won't taste the alcohol, but after two, you'll feel pretty good."

■ **The Iguana.** Mix equal parts of rum and vodka, and add either blue Curaçao or blue grenadine for color. Add crème de banane liqueur, coconut cream, and pineapple juice. Says Van Der Linde, "I learned this one more than 10 years ago on the first sailing boat I worked on. It was called the *Balia,* which means 'to dance.'"

■ **The Captain's Special.** Mix equal parts of rum and vodka, and add a splash of amaretto, crème de banane, and pineapple and orange juice. "It's really simple," says Van Der Linde, "just blend with crushed ice and it's ready to drink."

Holiday Inn Sunspree. Get your limbo on at this Wednesday-night party at the Iguana Pool Bar. The combination of a Caribbean buffet and flaming limbo performances makes for a lively evening. Overzealous diners needn't worry about their girth too much if they plan to give the limbo bar a try as it is literally raised much higher. ⊠ *J.E. Irausquin Blvd. 230, Palm Beach* ☎ *297/586–3600.*

SAN NICOLAS

BARS

Charlie's Bar. An Aruba institution since 1941, Charlie's is a bit far from most hotels, but certainly worth the trip. Expect a raucous and considerably soused crowd of good-natured folks. The food here is quite good as well, all the better for padding your stomach before the margaritas, but keep in mind that you may want to arrange a cab ride to this place if you're staying at a far-away hotel. ⊠ *Zeppenfeldstraat 56, San Nicolas* ☎ *297/584–5086.*

Cheta's Bar. Since 1948, Cheta's has been a real locals' joint. It holds no more than four customers at a time. There aren't any bar stools, either, which is why most patrons gather out front. ⊠ *Paradera 119, Paradera* ☎ *297/582–3689.*

Aruba has several art galleries where you can buy original paintings.

THE ARTS

Aruba has a handful of not-quite-famous but very talented stars. Over the years, several local artists, including composer Julio Renado Euson, choreographer Wilma Kuiperi, sculptor Ciro Abath, and visual artist Elvis Lopez, have gained international renown. Further, many Aruban musicians play more than one type of music (classical, jazz, soca, salsa, reggae, calypso, rap, pop), and many compose as well as perform.

The Union of Cultural Organizations is devoted to developing local art while broadening its international appeal. UNOCA provides scholarships to help artists of all ages to participate in exhibitions, shows, and festivals. Although some internationally recognized stars have returned to Aruba to help promote the island's cultural growth, renowned conductor and pianist Eldin Juddan says the island needs to do more to promote local musicians. "There's a lot of talent, but professional guidance is needed to bring these talents and music to their potential."

Cas Di Cultura. The National Theater of Aruba hosts art exhibits, folkloric shows, dance performances, and concerts throughout the year. ⊠ *Vondellaan 2, Oranjestad* ☎ *297/582–1010* ⊕ *www.casdicultura.aw*.

Further, the island's many festivals showcase arts and culture. To find out what's going on, check out *Aruba Today,*

CLOSE UP

Carnival

Aruba's biggest bash incorporates local traditions with those of Venezuela, Brazil, Holland, and North America. The festival was introduced to the island by Trinidadians who had come to work at the oil refinery in the 1940s. In Aruba, Carnival consists of six weeks of jump-ups (traditional Caribbean street celebrations), competitions, parties, and colorful parades. The celebrations culminate with the Grand Parade held in Oranjestad on the Sunday before Ash Wednesday. It lasts for hours and turns the streets into one big stage. The two main events are the Grand Children's Parade, where kids dress in colorful costumes and decorate floats, and the Lightning Parade, consisting of miles of glittery floats and lavish costumes. Steel-pan and brass bands supply the music that inspires the crowds to dance. All events end on Shrove Tuesday: at midnight an effigy of King Momo (traditionally depicted as a fat man) is burned, indicating the end of joy and the beginning of Lenten penitence.

6

the local newspaper, or *Calalou,* a Caribbean publication dedicated to the visual arts. You can also phone the national library, which has a bulletin board of events.

ART GALLERIES

Gasparito Restaurant & Art Gallery. A permanent exhibition by a variety of Aruban artists is featured here ranging from colorful landscapes to more abstract offerings. ⊠ *Gasparito 3, Noord* ☎ *297/586–7044.*

Insight Art Studio. Owner Alida Martinez, a Venezuelan-born artist, likes more-avant-garde displays, so don't expect to find the usual paintings of pastel-color skies here. Inventive works by local and international artists are featured. Martinez's own mixed-media creations juxtapose erotic and religious themes. The space, which includes a studio, is a magnet for the island's art community. Viewing is by appointment only. ⊠ *Paradera Park 215, Paradera* ☎ *297/582–5882.*

FESTIVALS

ANNUAL EVENTS

Caribbean Sea Jazz Festival. For a few nights each October you can hear jazz and Latin music performed at the outdoor venue next to the Renaissance Aruba Beach Resort at Renaissance Mall. ✉ *Cas di Cultura, Oranjestad* ⊕ *www. caribbeanseajazz.com.*

Carubbian Festival. Held most Thursdays from 6 to 10 pm, this family-friendly festival turns San Nicolas's Main Street into a party full of Aruban music, street food, culture, and booths selling handicrafts. Hotel packages to the festival, which include round-trip bus transportation, cost about $50. ✉ *Main Street, San Nicolas.*

The Dande Stroll. New Year's Eve is a big deal in most places, but on Aruba the fireworks that light up the sky at midnight are just the beginning. The Dande Stroll continues throughout New Year's Day. Groups of musicians stroll from house to house, singing good-luck greetings for the New Year. A prize is awarded to the group with the best song, which is sung by islanders during the next 12 months. Dande, by the way, comes from the Papiamento word "dandara," which means "to have a good time."

National Anthem & Flag Day. On March 18, an official holiday, you can stop by Plaza Betico Croes in Oranjestad for folkloric presentations and other traditional festivities.

St. John's Day. Also known as Dera Gai, the annual "burying of the rooster" festival is celebrated June 24 (the feast of St. John the Baptist). Festive songs, bright yellow-and-red costumes, and traditional dances mark this holiday dating from 1862. Today, the rooster—which symbolizes a successful harvest—has been replaced by a gourd.

CASINOS

AMONG THE BIGGEST DRAWS in Aruba are the island's elaborate, pulsating casinos. Aruba offers up gambling venues closer in spirit and form to Las Vegas than any other island in the Caribbean. Perhaps it's the predominantly American crowd, but the casinos remain busy and popular, and almost every big resort has one. Although people don't dress up as elegantly as they did in years gone by, most of the casinos still expect a somewhat more put-together look (in the evening, at least) than a T-shirt and flip-flops.

There was a time when women dressed in evening gowns and men donned suits for a chic, glamorous night in Aruba's casinos. In the mid-'80s, however, the Alhambra Casino opened, touting its philosophy of "barefoot elegance." Suddenly shorts and T-shirts became acceptable attire. The relaxed dress code made gaming seem an affordable pastime rather than a luxury.

Aruba's casinos now attract high rollers, low-stakes bettors, and nongamblers alike. Games include slot machines, blackjack (both beloved by North Americans), baccarat (preferred by South Americans), craps, roulette—even betting on sports events. Theaters, restaurants, bars, and cigar shops have added another dimension to the casinos. Now you can go out for dinner, take in a show, sip after-dinner drinks, and play blackjack all under one roof. In between games you can get to know other patrons and swap tips and tales. The many local entertainers who rotate among the casinos add to the excitement.

GAMBLING PRIMER

For a short-form handbook on the rules, the odds, and the strategies for the most popular casino games—or for help deciding on the kind of action that suits your style—read on.

THE GOOD BETS

The first part of any viable casino strategy is to risk the most money on wagers that present the lowest edge for the house. Blackjack, craps, video poker, and baccarat are the most advantageous to the bettor in this regard. The two types of bets at baccarat have a house advantage of a little more than 1%. The basic line bets at craps, if backed up with full odds, can be as low as 0.5%. Blackjack and video poker, at times, have a house edge that's less than

The Casablanca Casino in the Westin Aruba.

1% (nearly a 50–50 proposition), and with bettor diligence can actually present a slight long-term advantage.

How can a casino possibly provide you with a potentially positive expectation at some of its games? First, because a vast number of gamblers make the bad bets (those with a house advantage of 5%–35%, such as roulette, keno, and slots) day in and day out. Second, because the casino knows that very few people are aware of the opportunities to beat the odds. Third, because it takes skill—requiring study and practice—to be in a position to exploit these opportunities the casino presents. However, a mere hour or two spent learning strategies for the beatable games will put you light years ahead of the vast majority of visitors who give the gambling industry an average 12% to 15% profit margin.

THE GAMES

BACCARAT

The most "glamorous" game in the casino, baccarat is a version of *chemin de fer,* which is popular in European gambling halls. It's a favorite with high rollers because thousands of dollars are often staked on one hand. The Italian word *baccara* means "zero." This refers to the point value of 10s and picture cards. The game is run by four pit personnel. Two dealers sit side by side at the middle of the table. They handle the winning and losing bets and keep track of each player's "commission" *(explained below)*. The caller stands in the middle of the other side of the table and dictates the action. The "ladderman" supervises the game and acts as final judge if any disputes arise.

HOW TO PLAY

Baccarat is played with eight decks of cards dealt from a large "shoe" (or cardholder). Each player is offered a turn at handling the shoe and dealing the cards. Two two-card hands are dealt facedown: the "player" and the "bank" hands. The player who deals the cards is called the banker, although the house banks both hands. The players bet on which hand—player or banker—will come closest to adding up to 9 (a "natural"). Ace through 9 retain face value, and 10s and picture cards are worth zero. If you have a hand adding up to more than 10, the number 10 is subtracted from the total. For example, if one hand contains a 10 and a 4, the hand adds up to 4. If the other holds an ace and a 6, it adds up to 7. If a hand has a 7 and a 9, it adds up to 6.

Depending on the two hands, the caller either declares a winner and loser (if either hand actually adds up to 8 or 9) or calls for another card for the player hand (if it totals 1, 2, 3, 4, 5, or 10). The bank hand then either stands pat or draws a card, determined by a complex series of rules depending on what the player's total is and dictated by the caller. When one or the other hand is declared a winner, the dealers go into action to pay off the winning wagers, collect the losing wagers, and add up the commission (usually 5%) that the house collects on the bank hand. Both bets have a house advantage of slightly more than 1%.

The player-dealer (or banker) holds the shoe as long as the bank hand wins. When the player hand wins, the shoe moves counterclockwise around the table. Players can refuse the shoe and pass it to the next player. Because the caller dictates the action, player responsibilities are minimal. It's not necessary to know the card-drawing rules, even if you're the banker.

BACCARAT STRATEGY

To bet, you only have to place your money in the bank, player, or tie box on the layout, which appears directly in front of where you sit. If you're betting that the bank hand will win, you put your chips in the bank box; bets for the player hand go in the player box. (Only real suckers bet on the tie.) Most players bet on the bank hand when they deal, since they "represent" the bank and to do otherwise would seem as if they were betting "against" themselves. This isn't really true, but it seems that way. Playing baccarat is a simple matter of guessing whether the player or banker hand will come closest to 9 and deciding how much to bet on the outcome.

BLACKJACK

HOW TO PLAY

You play blackjack against a dealer, and whichever of you comes closest to a card total of 21 wins. Number cards are worth their face value, picture cards are worth 10, and aces are worth either 1 or 11. (Hands with aces are known as "soft" hands. Always count the ace first as an 11. If you also have a 10, your total will be 21, not 11.) If the dealer has a 17 and you have a 16, you lose. If you have an 18 against a dealer's 17, you win (even money). If both you and the dealer have a 17, it's a tie (or "push") and no money changes hands. If you go over a total of 21 (or "bust"), you lose, even if the dealer also busts later in the hand. If your first two cards add up to 21 (a "natural"), you're paid 3 to 2. However, if the dealer also has a natural, it's a push. A natural beats a total of 21 achieved with more than two cards.

7

You're dealt two cards, either facedown or faceup, depending on the custom of the casino. The dealer also gives herself two cards, one facedown and one faceup (except in double-exposure blackjack, where both the dealer's cards are visible). Depending on your first two cards and the dealer's up card, you can **stand,** or refuse to take another card. You can **hit,** or take as many cards as you need until you stand or bust. You can **double down,** or double your bet and take one card. You can **split** a like pair; if you're dealt two 8s, for example, you can double your bet and play the 8s as if they're two hands. You can **buy insurance** if the dealer is showing an ace. Here you're wagering half your initial bet that the dealer *does* have a natural. If so, you lose your initial bet but are paid 2 to 1 on the insurance (which means the whole thing is a push). You can **surrender** half your initial bet if you're holding a bad hand (known as a "stiff") such as a 15 or 16 against a high-up card such as a 9 or 10.

BLACKJACK STRATEGY

Many people devote a great deal of time to learning complicated statistical schemes. However, if you don't have the time, energy, or inclination to get that seriously involved, the following basic strategies should allow you to play the game with a modicum of skill and a paucity of humiliation:

When your hand is a total of 12, 13, 14, 15, or 16, and the dealer shows a 2, 3, 4, 5, or 6, you should stand. *Exception:* If your hand totals 12, and the dealer shows a 2 or 3, you should hit.

When your hand totals 12, 13, 14, 15, or 16, and the dealer shows a 7, 8, 9, 10, or ace, always hit.

When you hold 17, 18, 19, or 20, always stand.

When you hold a 10 or 11 and the dealer shows a 2, 3, 4, 5, 6, 7, 8, or 9, always double down.

When you hold a pair of aces or a pair of 8s, always split.

Never buy insurance.

CRAPS

Craps is a fast-paced, action-packed dice game that can require up to four pit personnel to run. Two dealers handle the bets made on either side of the layout. A "stickman" wields the long wooden stick, curved at one end, which is used to move the dice around the table. The stickman also calls the number that's rolled and books the proposition bets made in the middle of the layout. The "boxman" sits between the two dealers, overseeing the game and settling any disputes.

HOW TO PLAY

Stand at the table wherever you can find an open space. You can start betting casino chips immediately, but you have to wait your turn to be the shooter. The dice are passed clockwise around the table (the stickman will give you the dice at the appropriate time). It's important, when you're the shooter, to roll the dice hard enough so they bounce off the end wall of the table. This shows that you're not trying to control the dice with a "soft roll."

CRAPS STRATEGY

Playing craps is fairly straightforward; it's the betting that's complicated. The basic concepts are as follows: If the first time the shooter rolls the dice he or she turns up a 7 or 11, that's called a "natural"—an automatic win. If a 2, 3,

DID YOU KNOW?

Aruba offers the closest thing in the Caribbean to Las Vegas–style casino action, with some casinos in large hotels open 24 hours a day; the legal age for gambling is 18.

or 12 comes up on the first throw (called the "come-out roll"), that's termed "craps"—an automatic lose. Each of the numbers 4, 5, 6, 8, 9, or 10 on a first roll is known as a "point": the shooter keeps rolling the dice until the point comes up again. If a 7 turns up before the point does, that's another loser. When either the point or a losing 7 is rolled, this is known as a "decision," which happens on average every 3.3 rolls.

But "winning" and "losing" rolls of the dice are entirely relative in this game, because there are two ways you can bet at craps: "for" the shooter or "against" the shooter. Betting for means that the shooter will "make his point" (win). Betting against means that the shooter will "seven out" (lose). Either way, you're actually betting against the house, which books all wagers. If you're betting "for" on the come-out, you place your chips on the layout's "pass line." If a 7 or 11 is rolled, you win even money. If a 2, 3, or 12 (craps) is rolled, you lose your bet. If you're betting "against" on the come-out, you place your chips in the "don't pass bar." A 7 or 11 loses; a 2, 3, or 12 wins. A shooter can bet for or against himself, or against other players.

There are also roughly two dozen wagers you can make on any single specific roll of the dice. Craps strategy books can give you the details on come/don't come, odds, place, buy, big six, field, and proposition bets.

ROULETTE

Roulette is a casino game that uses a perfectly balanced wheel with 38 numbers (0, 00, and 1 through 36), a small white ball, a large layout with 11 different betting options, and special "wheel chips." The layout organizes 11 different bets into 6 "inside bets" (the single numbers, or those closest to the dealer) and 5 "outside bets" (the grouped bets, or those closest to the players).

The dealer spins the wheel clockwise and the ball counterclockwise. When the ball slows, the dealer announces, "No more bets." The ball drops from the "back track" to the "bottom track," caroming off built-in brass barriers and bouncing in and out of the different cups in the wheel before settling into the cup of the winning number. Then the dealer places a marker on the number and scoops all the losing chips into her corner. Depending on how crowded the game is, the casino can count on roughly 50 spins of the wheel per hour.

HOW TO PLAY

To buy in, place your cash on the layout near the wheel. Inform the dealer of the denomination of the individual unit you intend to play. Know the table limits (displayed on a sign in the dealer area). Don't ask for a 25¢ denomination if the minimum is $1. The dealer gives you a stack of wheel chips of a color that's different from those of all the other players and places a chip marker atop one of your wheel chips on the rim of the wheel to identify its denomination. Note that you must cash in your wheel chips at the roulette table before you leave the game. Only the dealer can verify how much they're worth.

ROULETTE STRATEGY

With **inside bets**, you can lay any number of chips (depending on the table limits) on a single number, 1 through 36 or 0 or 00. If the number hits, your payoff is 35 to 1, for a return of $36. You could, conceivably, place a $1 chip on all 38 numbers, but the return of $36 would leave you $2 short, which divides out to 5.26%, the house advantage. If you place a chip on the line between two numbers and one of those numbers hits, you're paid 17 to 1 for a return of $18 (again, $2 short of the true odds). Betting on three numbers returns 11 to 1, four numbers returns 8 to 1, five numbers pays 6 to 1 (this is the worst bet at roulette, with a 7.89% disadvantage), and six numbers pays 5 to 1.

To place an **outside bet**, lay a chip on one of three "columns" at the lower end of the layout next to numbers 34, 35, and 36. This pays 2 to 1. A bet placed in the first 12, second 12, or third 12 boxes also pays 2 to 1. A bet on red or black, odd or even, and 1 through 18 or 19 through 36 pays off at even money, 1 to 1. If you think you can bet on red *and* black, or odd *and* even, in order to play roulette and drink for free all night, think again. The green 0 or 00, which fall outside these two basic categories, will come up on average once every 19 spins of the wheel.

SLOT MACHINES

HOW TO PLAY

Playing slots is basically the same as it's always been. But the look and feel of the games has changed dramatically in the last several years. Machines that used to dispense a noisy waterfall of coins have all but given way to new generations of machines that payout wins with printed coded tickets instead of coins. If you are a historian, or sentimental, you can still find a few coin-dispensing relics, but in

Craps at the Crystal Casino in the Renaissance Aruba.

the larger casinos they've almost all been replaced by the new ticketing payout system. These tickets can be inserted into other slot machines like cash, or can be redeemed at the Cage or at ATM-like machines that dispense cash right on the casino floor. Nowadays many of the games are all-digital, with touch screens, and play like video games. But the underlying concept is still the same: after you start the game, you're looking for the reels—real or virtual—to match a winning pattern of shapes.

SLOT-MACHINE STRATEGY
The house advantage on slots varies from machine to machine, between 3% and 25%. Casinos that advertise a 97% payback are telling you that at least one of their slot machines has a house advantage of 3%. Which one? There's really no way of knowing. Generally, $1 machines pay back at a higher percentage than 25¢ or 5¢ machines. On the other hand, machines with smaller jackpots pay back more money more frequently, meaning that you'll be playing with more of your winnings.

One of the all-time great myths about slot machines is that they're "due" for a jackpot. Slots, like roulette, craps, keno, and Big Six, are subject to the Law of Independent Trials, which means the odds are permanently and unalterably fixed. If the odds of lining up three sevens on a 25¢ slot machine have been set by the casino at 1 in 10,000, then those odds remain 1 in 10,000 whether the three 7s have been hit three times in a row or not hit for 90,000 plays. Don't waste a lot of time playing a machine that you suspect is "ready," and don't think if someone hits a jackpot on a particular machine only minutes after you've finished playing on it that it was "yours."

VIDEO POKER
This section deals only with straight-draw video poker.

Like blackjack, video poker is a game of strategy and skill, and at select times on select machines the player actually holds the advantage, however slight, over the house. Unlike with slot machines, you can determine the exact edge of video-poker machines. Like slots, however, video-poker machines are often tied into a progressive meter; when the jackpot total reaches high enough, you can beat the casino at its own game. The variety of video-poker machines is growing steadily. All are played in similar fashion, but the strategies are different.

HOW TO PLAY
The schedule for the payback on winning hands is posted on the machine, usually above the screen. It lists the returns for a high pair (generally jacks or better), two pair, three of a kind, a flush, full house, straight flush, four of a kind, and royal flush, depending on the number of coins played—usually 1, 2, 3, 4, or 5. Look for machines that pay with a single coin played: 1 coin for "jacks or better" (meaning a pair of jacks, queens, kings, or aces; any other pair is a stiff), 2 coins for two pairs, 3 for three of a kind, 6 for a flush, 9 for a full house, 50 for a straight flush, 100 for four of a kind, and 250 for a royal flush. This is known as a 9/6 machine—one that gives a nine-coin payback for a full house and a six-coin payback for a flush with one coin played. Other machines are known as 8/5 (eight for a full house, five for a flush), 7/5, and 6/5.

You want a 9/6 machine because it gives you the best odds: the return from a standard 9/6 straight-draw machine is 99.5%; you give up only half a percent to the house. An 8/5 machine returns 97.3%. On 6/5 machines, the figure drops to 95.1%, slightly less than roulette. Machines with varying paybacks are scattered throughout the casinos. In some you'll see an 8/5 machine right next to a 9/6, and someone will be blithely playing the 8/5 machine.

As with slot machines, it's optimum to play the maximum number of coins to qualify for the jackpot. You insert five coins into the slot and press the "deal" button. Five cards appear on the screen—say, 5, jack, queen, 5, 9. To hold the pair of 5s, you press the hold buttons under the first and fourth cards. The word "hold" appears underneath the two 5s. You then press the "draw" button (often the same button as "deal") and three new cards appear on the screen—say, 10, jack, 5. You have three 5s. With five coins bet, the machine will give you 15 credits. Now you can press the "max bet" button: five units will be removed from your credits, and five new cards will appear on the screen. You repeat the hold-and-draw process; if you hit a winning hand, the proper payback will be added to your credits.

VIDEO-POKER STRATEGY

Like blackjack, video poker has a basic strategy that's been formulated by the computer simulation of hundreds of millions of hands. The most effective way to learn it is with a video poker–computer program that deals the cards on your screen, then tutors you in how to play each hand properly. If you don't want to devote that much time to the study of video poker, memorizing these six rules will help you make the right decision for more than half the hands you'll be dealt:

If you're dealt a completely "stiff" hand (no like cards and no picture cards), draw five new cards.

If you're dealt a hand with no like cards but with one jack, queen, king, or ace, always hold on to the picture card; if you're dealt two different picture cards, hold both. But if you're dealt three different picture cards, hold only two (the two of the same suit, if that's an option).

If you're dealt a pair, hold it, no matter the face value.

Never hold a picture card with a pair of 2s through 10s.

Never draw two cards to try for a straight or a flush.

Never draw one card to try for an inside straight.

The Copacabana Casino at the Hyatt Regency Aruba.

THE CASINOS

Most casinos are found in hotels; all are along Palm Beach or Eagle Beach or in downtown Oranjestad. Although the minimum age to enter is 18, some venues are relaxed about this rule. By day "barefoot elegance" is the norm in all casinos, although many establishments have a shirt-and-shoes requirement. Evening dress is expected to be more polished, though still casual. In high season the casinos are open from just before noon to the wee hours; in low season (May to November) they may not start dealing until late afternoon.

If you plan to play large sums of money, check in with the casino upon arrival so that you can be rewarded for your business. Most hotels offer gambling goodies—complimentary meals at local restaurants, chauffeured tours, and, in the cases of big spenders, high-roller suites. Even small-scale gamblers may be entitled to coupons for meals and discounted rooms.

ORANJESTAD AND ENVIRONS

Alhambra Casino. Amid the Spanish-style arches and leaded glass, you can try your luck at blackjack, Caribbean stud poker, three-card poker, roulette, craps, or one of the 300 slot machines that accept American nickels, quarters, and dollars. A casual atmosphere and $5 tables further the welcoming feel. Head to one of the novelty touch-screen machines, each of which has a variety of games. There's also bingo every Saturday, Monday, and Thursday beginning at 1 pm. If you fill your card, you can collect the grand prize of a few hundred dollars—not bad for a $5 investment. Be sure to sign up for the Alhambra Advantage Card, which gives you a point for each dollar you spend—even if you lose at the tables, you can still go home with prizes. Of course, winners can spend their earnings immediately at the many on-site shops. The casino is owned by the Divi resorts, and golf carts run to and from nearby hotels every 15 minutes or so. The slots here open daily at 10 am; gaming tables operate from 6 pm until 4 am. It can get quite smoky sometimes. ⊠ *L.G. Smith Blvd. 47, Oranjestad* ☎ *297/583–5000* ⊕ *www.casinoalhambra.com.*

Crystal Casino. Adorned with Austrian crystal chandeliers and gold-leaf columns, the Renaissance Aruba's glittering casino evokes Monaco's grand establishments. The Salon Privé offers serious gamblers a private room for baccarat, roulette, and high-stakes blackjack. This casino is popular among cruise-ship passengers, who stroll over from the port to watch and play in slot tournaments and bet on sporting events. The Crystal Lounge, which overlooks the betting floor, offers live music along with cocktails. ⊠ *Renaissance Aruba Resort & Casino, L.G. Smith Blvd. 82, Oranjestad* ☎ *297/583–6000.*

Seaport Casino. The low-key gambling here is at a waterside location adjacent to the Renaissance conference center, Beach Tower, and Marketplace. More than 200 slot machines are in daily operation from 10 am to 4 am, and tables are open from 4 pm to 4 am. From here you can see the boats on the ocean and enjoy not only the games you'd find at other casinos but also shops, restaurants, bars, and movie theaters. Stop by on Tuesday, Thursday, or Sunday for the casino's popular bingo tournaments. ⊠ *L.G. Smith Blvd. 9, Oranjestad* ☎ *297/583–6000.*

PALM BEACH AND NOORD

The Casino at the Radisson Aruba Resort. Although it measures 16,000 square feet, this casino takes a bit of seeking out. Descend the stairs at the corner of the resort's lobby, following the sounds of the piano player's tunes. The nightly action here includes Las Vegas–style blackjack, roulette, craps, and slot machines. Overhead, thousands of lights

Good-Luck Charms

Arubans take myths and superstitions very seriously. They flinch if a black butterfly flits into their home, because this symbolizes death. They gasp if a child crawls under their legs, because it's a sign that the baby won't grow anymore. And on New Year's Eve they toss the first sips of whiskey, rum, or champagne from the first bottle that's opened in the New Year out the door of their house to show respect to those who have died and to wish luck on others. It's no surprise, then, that good-luck charms are part of Aruba's ca-

sino culture as well.

The island's most common good-luck charm is the *djucu* (pronounced *joo*-koo), a brown-and-black stone that comes from the sea and becomes hot when rubbed. Many people have them put in gold settings—with their initials engraved in the metal—and wear them around their necks on a chain with other charms such as an anchor or a cross. Another item that's thought to bring good luck is a small bag of sand. Women wear them tucked discreetly into their bras.

---

simulate shooting stars. A host of shops and restaurants let you chip away at your newfound wealth. The slots here open daily at noon, and the table action begins at 6 pm. Everything shuts down at 4 am. ⊠ *Radisson Aruba Resort & Casino, J.E. Irausquin Blvd. 81, Palm Beach* ☎ *297/586–4045.*

Excelsior Casino. The Excelsior, the birthplace of Caribbean stud, also offers blackjack, craps, and roulette tables; plenty of slot machines; and a bar featuring live entertainment. There's also a poker room for Texas hold 'em, seven-card stud, and Caribbean stud. The casino has seen better days but is open daily from 8 am to 4 am; slots begin spinning at 9 am, and tables open at 12:30 pm. ⊠ *Holiday Inn Resort Aruba, J.E. Irausquin Blvd. 230, Palm Beach* ☎ *297/586– 7777, 297/586–3600* ⊕ *www.excelsiorcasino.com.*

Hyatt Regency Casino. Ablaze with neon, this hotel casino is an enormous complex with a Carnival-in-Rio theme. The most popular games here are slots, blackjack, craps, and baccarat. Slots and some other games are available at noon, the dice start rolling at 6 pm, and all other pursuits are open by 8 pm. From 9 pm to 2 am there's live music at the stage near the bar—you'll find it hard to steal away

The Seaport Casino is the only Aruba casino on the waterfront.

from the pulsating mix of Latin and American tunes. You can register for free dinners and brunches and hotel discounts at the hostess station. The casino is open until 4 am. ✉ *Hyatt Regency Aruba Beach Resort & Casino, J.E. Irausquin Blvd. 85, Palm Beach* ☎ *297/586–1234* ⊕ *www.aruba.hyatt.com.*

Palm Beach Casino. The Westin's casino is all about sophistication. Spend some time at the five Hyperlink machines, blackjack, roulette, craps, Caribbean poker, and baccarat tables, or at one of the 300 slot machines. If gambling isn't your style, visit the bar for exotic cocktails and live entertainment most nights at 9. ✉ *Westin Aruba Resort, Spa & Casino, J.E. Irausquin Blvd. 77, Palm Beach* ☎ *297/586–4466* ⊕ *www.westinaruba.com* ⊗ *Noon–4 am.*

The Riu Palace Casino. With a preponderance of dark woods and lavish fabrics, the Rui Palace tends toward opulence. Though not the largest casino on the island, it does have blackjack and baccarat tables, slots, roulette, and cocktails galore. ✉ *J.E. Irausquin Blvd. 79, Palm Beach* ☎ *297/586–3900.*

The Royal Palm Casino. The Occidental Grand Aruba's casino opens daily at noon for slots and at 5 pm for all other games. Famous movie stars gaze down at you from a 30-foot mural as you take your chances at one of 245 slots or at dozens of blackjack, roulette, poker, craps, baccarat, and Caribbean stud poker tables. The entire gaming floor joins in the free full-card bingo game held nightly at 10:30. Anyone who scores a full card within the first 50 calls wins a clean grand; everyone who shows a full card after that walks away with $100. There's a slot tournament every Friday at 8 pm, and look for double jackpots daily from 3 to 5 pm. The nightly bingo game always draws a crowd with a jackpot of $2,000. You can hang around until 4 am. ⊠ *Occidental Grand Aruba, J.E. Irausquin Blvd. 83, Palm Beach* ☎ *297/586–9039* ⊕ *www. occidentalhotels.com.*

Stellaris Casino. Mirrors on the ceilings reflect the glamorous chandeliers at this 24-hour facility. Take your pick between craps, roulette, Caribbean stud poker, minibaccarat, and superbuck (like blackjack with suits). Every night except Sunday there's a performance by musician Cesar Olarta that may boost your luck. Check in with the casino when you arrive at the hotel and you can get a membership card. If you play high enough stakes at the tables, you can win free meals and other prizes. If not, you can at least get a postcard in the mail offering a special rate on future stays. The hotel offers a 30% discount to those who play at least four hours each day. This is the largest casino on the island. ⊠ *Aruba Marriott Resort, L.G. Smith Blvd. 101, Palm Beach* ☎ *297/586–9000.*

Trop Club & Casino. Billed as a boutique casino, the Trop Club offers plentiful slot opportunities in an intimate and comfortable environment. Though the table games are limited, players of blackjack and roulette should have more than enough to keep them happy. ⊠ *Tropicana Aruba Resort & Casino, J.E. Irausquin Blvd. 248, Eagle Beach* ☎ *297/587– 9000* ⊕ *www.troparuba.com.*

SPORTS
AND THE
OUTDOORS

Relatively flat, Aruba is the perfect biking destination.

Above the surface and below, Aruban waters are brimming with activity. Although beach bumming is a popular pastime, golf, tennis, and horseback riding are also good options. More adventurous souls can explore the terrain on a motorcycle, parasail through the Aruban sky, or harness the power of the wind on a kiteboard. Constant trade winds have made Aruba an internationally recognized windsurfing destination. The crystalline waters of the island's leeward side offer scuba divers and snorkelers a kaleidoscopic adventure day or night.

BIKING AND MOTORCYCLING

Biking is a great way to get around the island; the climate is perfect, and the trade winds help keep you cool. If you prefer to exert less energy while reaping the rewards of the outdoors, a scooter is a great way to whiz from place to place. Or let your hair down completely and cruise around on a Harley-Davidson.

ORGANIZED EXCURSIONS

Big Twin Aruba. Live the dream: Rent a Hog and tour Aruba! With an initial $2,500 deposit if renting to adventure on your own, or $1,000 down if joining the organized tour, rates are $175 for a day or $140 for a half day (including insurance and helmets). The dealership also sells Harley clothing, accessories, and collectibles. Be sure to pose for a photo next to the classic 1939 Liberator on display in the showroom. The shop is open Monday through Saturday from 9 to 6. ✉ *L.G. Smith Blvd. 124A, Oranjestad* ☎ *297/582–8660* ⊕ *www.harleydavidson-aruba.com.*

Kini Kini Transfer and Tours. Head to Kini Kini for four-hour guided tours using all-terrain vehicles that explore the rugged North coast. Prices per vehicle range from $110 for a solo ride to $130 for a driver plus passenger. Private tours are also available. ✉ *Flacciusstraat 33, Oranjestad* ☎ *297/588–3333* ⊕ *www.kinikinitours.com.*

Rancho Notorious. Exciting mountain-biking tours are available here. The 2½-hour tour to the Alto Vista Chapel and the California Lighthouse are $50 ($75 with bike rental). ✉ *Boroncana, Noord* ☎ *297/586–0508* ⊕ *www.ranchonotorious.com.*

RENTALS

There are plenty of dealers who will be happy to help you in your motoring pursuits.

Donata Car and Cycle. Rent motorcycles and mopeds here. ✉ *Catiri 59, Oranjestad* ☎ *297/587–6291.*

George's Cycle Center. Goerges has been renting motorcycles, scooters, and all-terrain vehicles for more than 30 years. ✉ *L.G. Smith Blvd. 136, Oranjestad* ☎ *297/592–5875* ⊕ *www.georgecycles.com.*

Pablito's Bike & Locker Rental. Mountain bikes are available here for $25 a day. ✉ *L.G. Smith Blvd. 234, Oranjestad* ☎ *297/587–0047.*

Semver Cycle Rental. The staff here can help you choose the motorcycle or scooter that matches your experience level and your plans for the day. ✉ *Noord 22, Noord* ☎ *297/586–6851* ⊕ *www.semver.aw/semvercyclerentalhomepage.htm.*

BOWLING

FAMILY **Eagle Bowling Palace.** The Eagle has 16 lanes, a snack bar, and a cocktail lounge. It's open Monday and Tuesday from 5 pm to 1 am; Sunday, Wednesday, and Thursday from 10 am to 1 am; and on Friday and Saturday from 10 am to 2 am. Children under 12 can bowl until 7 pm. One lane for one hour will cost $14 to $17, depending on the time of day. ✉ *Sasakiweg, Pos Abou, Oranjestad* ☎ *297/583–5038.*

Snorkeling from a replica pirate ship

DAY SAILS

If you plan to take a cruise around the island, know that the trade winds can make the waters choppy, and that catamaran rides are much smoother than those on single-hull boats. Sucking on a peppermint or ginger candy may soothe your queasy stomach; avoid boating with an empty or overly full stomach. Moonlight cruises cost about $45 per person. There are also a variety of snorkeling, dinner and dancing, and sunset party cruises to choose from, priced from $30 to $60 per person. Many of the smaller operators work out of their homes; they often offer to pick you up (and drop you off) at your hotel or meet you at a particular hotel pier.

Mi Dushi. This romantic, two-masted ship ("My Sweetheart") offers daytime snorkeling trips that include breakfast, lunch, and drinks for $59 per person. It also offers popular sunset happy-hour cruises *(see ⇨ Cruises in Chapter 5, Nightlife)*. ⊠ *Turibana Plaza, Noord 124, Noord* ☎ *297/586–2010* ⊕ *www.midushi.com.*

Octopus Sailing Charters. The drinks flow freely on Octopus's trimaran. It holds about 20 people for a three-hour afternoon sail, which costs $35. ⊠ *Pelican Pier, Palm Beach* ☎ *297/586–4281* ⊕ *www.octopusaruba.com.*

Seaport Marina. This is the place to go for charters. ⊠ *Renaissance Marketplace 204, Oranjestad.*

'Go On with the Struggle'

Arubans are proud of their autonomous standing within the Kingdom of the Netherlands, and Gilberto François "Betico" Croes is heralded as the hero behind the island's *status aparte* (separate status). His birthday, January 25, is an official Aruban holiday.

During the Dutch colonial expansion of the 17th century, Aruba and five other islands—Bonaire, Curaçao, St. Maarten, St. Eustatius, and Saba—became territories known as the Netherlands Antilles. After World War II these islands began to pressure Holland for autonomy, and in 1954 they became a collective self-governing entity under the umbrella of the Kingdom of the Netherlands.

At that time, several political parties were in power on the island. Soon, however, Juancho Irausquin (who has a major thoroughfare named in his honor) formed a new party that maintained control for nearly two decades. Irausquin was considered the founder of Aruba's new economic order and the precursor of modern Aruban politics. After his death his party's power diminished.

In 1971 Croes, then a young, ambitious school administrator, became the leader of another political party. Bolstered by a thriving economy generated by Aruba's oil refinery, Croes spearheaded the island's cause to secede from the Netherlands Antilles and to gain status as an equal partner within the Dutch kingdom. Sadly, he didn't live to celebrate the realization of his dream. On December 31, 1985, the day before Aruba's new status became official, Croes was in a car accident that put him in a coma for 11 months. He died on November 26, 1986. Etched in the minds of Arubans are his prophetic words: *"Si mi cai na cominda, gara e bandera y sigui cu e lucha"* ("If I die along the way, seize the flag and go on with the struggle").

Tranquilo Charters Aruba. Operated by Captain Hagedoorn, Tranquilo offers entertaining cruises, including a six-hour tour to the south side of the island for $75. Snorkeling equipment and free lessons are included in the package, and so is the very good "mom's Dutch pea soup" served with lunch (also included). ⊠ *Renaissance Marina, Oranjestad* ☎ *297/586–1418* ⊕ *www.tranquiloaruba.com.*

The California Lighthouse towers over Tierra del Sol golf course.

FISHING

Deep-sea catches here include barracuda, kingfish, wahoo, bonito, and black-and-yellow tuna. November to April is the catch-and-release season for sailfish and marlin. Many skippered charter boats are available for half- or full-day sails. Packages include tackle, bait, and refreshments. Prices range from $350 to $450 for a half-day charter and from $500 to $700 for a full day.

Teaser Charters. The expertise of the Teaser crew is matched by a commitment to sensible fishing practices, which include catch and release and avoiding ecologically sensitive areas. The company's two boats are fully equipped, and the crew seem to have an uncanny ability to locate the best fishing spots. Captain Kenny runs a thrilling expedition. ✉ *Renaissance Marina, Oranjestad* ☎ *297/582–5088* ⊕ *www.teasercharters.com.*

GOLF

Golf may seem incongruous on an arid island such as Aruba, yet there are several popular courses. Trade winds and the occasional stray goat add unexpected hazards.

Aruba Golf Club. This 9-hole course has 20 sand traps, five water traps, roaming goats, and lots of cacti. There are also 11 greens covered with artificial turf, making 18-hole tournaments a possibility. The clubhouse has a bar and

CLOSE UP

Sidney Ponson: Pitcher

When he was growing up in Aruba, Sidney Ponson loved sailing, scuba diving, and just about anything to do with the ocean. "My life was the beach," says Ponson, "before baseball." He started playing baseball when he was nine, even though the game was pretty difficult on an arid island where the fields are full of rocks. But employment on his uncle's boat taught him to work hard for what he wanted in life.

The pitcher signed with the minor leagues at 16, then was tapped by the Baltimore Orioles by the time he was 21. Hitting the big leagues involved lots of hard work (his grueling workouts last from 7:30 am to 1 pm and involve lifting weights, running, and throwing), but Ponson says it was worth it when he got the call to play. "It was 6:30 am, and I was on a road trip in a hotel in Scranton," he remembers. "They told me when to show up and said to be ready to play at 8:30."

Now Ponson is currently a free agent and spends much of his time in Aruba resting and visiting family and friends. Ponson used his status as a major leaguer to do some good for his island. He and fellow Aruban baseball player Calvin Maduro draft other professional baseball players, including Pedro Martinez and Manny Ramirez, to play in an annual celebrity softball game to raise funds for Aruba's Cas pa Hubentud, a home for underprivileged children.

He was awarded with the Order of Orange-Nassau by Queen Beatrix of the Netherlands in 2003.

8

locker rooms. Greens fees are $25 for 9 holes, $35 for 18 holes. Golf carts are available. ✉ *Golfweg 82, San Nicolas* ☎ *297/584–2006.*

The Links at Divi Aruba. Designed by Karl Litten and Lorie Viola, this 9-hole, par-36, paspalum-grass course (best for seaside courses) takes you past beautiful lagoons. Amenities include a golf school with professional instruction, a swing-analysis station, a driving range, and a two-story golf clubhouse with a pro shop. Two restaurants are available: Windows on Aruba for fine dining and Mulligan's for a casual and quick lunch. Greens fees are $90 for 9 holes, $129 for 18 from December to April; guests of the Divi properties get a discount. ✉ *Divi Aruba Resort, J.E. Irausquin Blvd. 93, Oranjestad* ☎ *297/581–4653.*

★ Fodor'sChoice **Tierra del Sol.** Designed by Robert Trent Jones Jr., this 18-hole championship course combines Aruba's native beauty—cacti and rock formations—with the lush greens of the world's best courses. The stunning course is on the northwest coast near the California Lighthouse. The greens fees vary depending on the time of day (from December to March it is $159 in the morning, $131 for early afternoon, and $100 from 3 pm). The fee includes a golf cart equipped with a communications system that allows you to order drinks for your return to the clubhouse. Half-day golf clinics, a bargain at $55, are available Monday, Tuesday, and Thursday. The pro shop is one of the Caribbean's most elegant, with an extremely attentive staff. ⊠ *Malmokweg* ☎ *297/586–0978.*

HIKING

Despite Aruba's arid landscape, hiking the rugged countryside will give you the best opportunities to see the island's wildlife and flora. Arikok National Wildlife Park is an excellent place to glimpse the real Aruba, free of the trappings of tourism. The heat can be oppressive, so be sure to take it easy, wear a hat, and have a bottle of water handy.

Arikok National Park. There are more than 34 km (20 miles) of trails concentrated in the island's eastern interior and along its northeastern coast. Arikok Park is crowned by Aruba's second-highest mountain, the 577-foot Mt. Arikok, so you can also go climbing here.

Hiking in the park, whether alone or in a group led by guides, is generally not too strenuous. Look for different colors to determine the degree of difficulty of each trail. You'll need sturdy shoes to grip the granular surfaces and climb the occasionally steep terrain. You should also exercise caution with the strong sun—bring along plenty of water and wear sunscreen and a hat. On the rare occasion that it rains, the park should be avoided completely, as mud makes both driving and hiking treacherous. At the park's main entrance, the Arikok Center houses offices, restrooms, and food facilities. All visitors must stop here upon entering, so that officials can manage the traffic flow and distribute information on park rules and features. ☎ *297/582–8001* ⊕ *www.arubanationalpark.org.*

FAMILY **Nature Sensitive Tours.** Eddy Croes, a former park ranger whose passion for the area is seemingly unbounded, runs this outfitter with care. Groups are never larger than eight

Horseback riding on the beach

people, so you'll see as much detail as you can handle. Expect frequent stops, when Eddy asks for silence so that you can hear the sounds of the park. The hikes are done at an easy pace and are suitable for basically anyone. A moonlight walk is available for those looking to avoid the heat. ✉ *Pos Chiquito 13E, Savaneta* ☎ *297/585–1594* ⊕ *www.naturesensitivetours.com.*

HORSEBACK RIDING

Ranches offer short jaunts along the beach or longer rides along trails passing through countryside flanked by cacti, divi-divi trees, and aloe vera plants. Ask if you can stop off at Cura di Tortuga, a natural pool that's reputed to have restorative powers. Rides are also possible in Arikok National Wildlife Park. Rates run from $35 for an hour-long trip to $65 for a three-hour tour; private rides cost slightly more.

FAMILY **Rancho Daimari.** Have your horse lead you to water—at the Natural Pool—in the morning or afternoon for $78 per person. The "Junior Dudes" program is tailored to young riders. There are also ATV trips. ✉ *Tanki Leendert 249, San Nicolas* ☎ *297/586–6284* ⊕ *www.arubaranchodaimari.com.*

Rancho Notorious. The one- to three-hour tours here include one to the countryside for $55 and a trip to the beach for $100. All skill levels are welcome. The company also organizes ATV and mountain-biking trips. ✉ *Boroncana, Noord* ☎ *297/586–0508* ⊕ *www.ranchonotorious.com.*

Kayaking in a sheltered cove

JET SKIING

If zipping through aqua-blue water at unholy speeds is your idea of fun, then renting a Jet Ski may be the way to go. Rentals are available in the water-sports centers at most hotels. Average prices for a half-hour ride are $65 for a single Jet Ski and $75 for a double. There are a few operators on the island, two of which are well regarded.

KAYAKING

Kayaking is a popular sport on Aruba, especially because the waters are so calm. It's a great way to explore the coast.

Aruba Watersport Center. Operating since 1960, Aruba Watersport offers both single and double kayaks. ⊠ *L.G. Smith Blvd. 81B, Noord* ☎ *297/586–6613*.

KITEBOARDING

Thanks to constant trade winds, kiteboarding (also called kitesurfing) is fast becoming a popular pastime on this tiny island. The sport involves gliding on and above the water on a small surfboard or wakeboard while hooked up to an inflatable kite. Windsurfing experience helps, and practice time on the beach is essential.

Aruba Active Vacations. Kiteboarding rental costs are usually $60 per day (though it may take the better part of a day

Wildlife Watching

Wildlife abounds on Aruba. Look for the cottontail rabbit: the black patch on its neck likens it to a species found in Venezuela, spawning a theory that it was brought to the island by pre-Columbian peoples. Wild donkeys, originally transported to the island by the Spanish, are found in the more rugged terrain; sheep and goats roam freely throughout the island.

About 170 bird species make their home on Aruba year-round, and migratory birds temporarily raise the total to 300 species when they fly by in November and January. Among the highlights are the *trupiaal* (bright orange), the *prikichi* (a parakeet with a green body and yellow head), and the *barika geel* (a small, yellow-bellied bird with a sweet tooth—you may find one eating the sugar off your breakfast table). At Bubali Bird Sanctuary, on the island's western side, you can see various types of waterfowl, especially cormorants, herons, scarlet ibis, and fish eagles. Along the south shore brown pelicans are common. At Tierra del Sol Golf Course in the north you may glimpse the *shoko,* the endangered burrowing owl.

Lizard varieties include large iguanas, once hunted for use in local soups and stews. (That practice is now illegal.) Like chameleons, these iguanas change color to adapt to their surroundings—from bright green when foraging in the foliage (which they love to eat) to a brownish shade when sunning themselves in the dirt. The *pega pega*—a cousin of the gecko—is named for the suction pads on its feet that allow it to grip virtually any surface (*pega* means "to stick" in Papiamento). The *kododo blauw* (whiptail lizard) is one of the species that's unique to the island.

Two types of snakes are found only on Aruba. The cat-eyed *santanero* isn't venomous, but it won't hesitate to defecate in your hand should you pick it up. The poisonous *cascabel* is a unique subspecies of rattlesnake that doesn't use its rattle. These snakes live in the area between Mt. Yamanota, Fontein, and San Nicolas.

8

to get the hang of it) with a $10 insurance charge. Once you're proficient, you may want to participate in some of the island's freestyle tournaments and long-distance races. Aruba Active Vacations is also a major windsurfing center on the island. ⊠ *North end of beach, Fisherman's Huts Beach* ☎ *297/586–0989* ⊕ *www.aruba-active-vacations.com.*

Fisherman's Huts Windsurf Center. Those eager to fly the friendly skies can take lessons and rent reliable equipment at Fisherman's Huts. ⊠ *L.G. Smith Blvd. 101, Palm Beach* ☎ *297/586–9000, 800/223–5443* ⊕ *www.velawindsurf.com.*

MULTISPORT OUTFITTERS

There are a number of outfitters in Aruba that can handle nearly all your water- or land-based activities with guided excursions and rental equipment. Here is a list of a few of our favorites.

De Palm Tours. This dependable operator has a near monopoly on Aruban sightseeing. The basic 3½-hour tour hits highlights of the island. Wear sneakers or hiking shoes, and bring a lightweight jacket or wrap, as the air-conditioned bus gets cold. De Palm also arranges horseback excursions.

You can also sail the open seas on a four-hour snorkeling adventure at nearby reefs. The cost for the catamaran trip is $78 per person, with a buffet lunch included. Tour departs from the De Palm Pier between the Riu and Radisson resorts. And De Palm is one of the best choices for your undersea experience; the options go beyond basic diving. Don a helmet and walk along the ocean floor near De Palm Island, home of huge blue parrot fish, or try Snuba—which is like scuba diving but without the heavy air tanks. A onehour snuba adventure costs $41. You can make reservations through its general office or at hotel tour-desk branches. ⊠ *L.G. Smith Blvd. 142, Oranjestad* ☎ *297/582–4400, 800/766–6016* ⊕ *www.depalm.com.*

Pelican Adventures. In operation since 1984, this company arranges sailing and boating charters for fishing and exploring, as well as jeep adventures and guided excursions to Aruba's caves and historic sites. Scuba and snorkeling trips are available for divers of all levels. Novices start with midmorning classes and then move to the pool to practice what they've learned; by afternoon they put their new skills to use at a shipwreck off the coast. Enjoy daytime snorkeling trips to two different reefs for about $47 per person. The company also offers sunset sails for $45 that can be combined with dinner at the Pelican Restaurant on Palm Beach. ⊠ *Pelican Pier, near Holiday Inn and Playa Linda hotels, Palm Beach* ☎ *297/586–3271* ⊕ *www.pelican-aruba.com.*

Red Sail Sports. Red Sail can arrange everything for your fishing trip. Choose between four catamarans, including the 70-foot *Rumba.* They offer a popular sunset sail, including drinks and a lively atmosphere for $49 per person; the dinner cruise package includes a three-course meal and open bar for $99. Red Sail Sports also has locations at the Hyatt and Marriott hotels. And though it's best known for its diving trips, Red Sail will also take you parasailing, and they offer courses for children and others new to scuba diving. An introductory class costs about $95. ✉ *J.E. Irausquin Blvd 348A, Palm Beach* ☎ *297/586–1603, 305/454–2538 in U.S.* ⊕ *www.redsailaruba.com.*

PARKS AND PLAYGROUNDS

FAMILY **Tira Koochi Park.** This playground, behind Prome Paso School, is open from 4 pm to 6:30 pm daily. ✉ *Savaneta 338A, Oranjestad.*

SCUBA DIVING AND SNORKELING

With visibility of up to 90 feet, the waters around Aruba are excellent for snorkeling and diving. Advanced and novice divers alike will find plenty to occupy their time, as many of the most popular sites—including some interesting shipwrecks—are found in shallow waters ranging from 30 to 60 feet. Coral reefs covered with sensuously waving sea fans and eerie giant sponge tubes attract a colorful menagerie of sea life, including gliding manta rays, curious sea turtles, shy octopuses, and fish from grunts to groupers. Marine preservation is a priority on Aruba, and regulations by the Conference on International Trade in Endangered Species make it unlawful to remove coral, conch, and other marine life from the water.

8

Expect snorkel gear to rent for about $15 per day and trips to cost around $40. Scuba rates are around $50 for a one-tank reef or wreck dive, $65 for a two-tank dive, and $45 for a night dive. Resort courses, which offer an introduction to scuba diving, average $65 to $70. If you want to go all the way, complete open-water certification costs around $350.

OPERATORS

Aruba Pro Dive. Experienced divers head here for good deals. ⊠ *Ponton 90, Noord* ☎ *297/582–5520* ⊕ *www.arubapro-dive.com.*

Dive Aruba. Resort courses, certification courses, and trips to interesting shipwrecks make Dive Aruba worth checking out. ⊠ *Wilhelminastraat 8, Oranjestad* ☎ *297/582–7337* ⊕ *www.divearuba.com.*

Native Divers Aruba. Underwater naturalist courses are taught by PADI-certified instructors here, and the company has legions of return customers. ⊠ *Marriott Surf Club, Palm Beach* ☎ *297/586–4763* ⊕ *www.nativedivers.com.*

SEAruba Fly 'n Dive. Aside from the usual diving courses, SEAruba can also instruct your group in rescue techniques and the finer points of underwater photography. ⊠ *L.G. Smith Blvd. 1A, Oranjestad* ☎ *297/587–8759* ⊕ *www.se-aruba.com.*

Unique Sports of Aruba. Dive master, rescue, and certification courses are offered at this operator, which lives up to its name. Single and double Jet Skis are also available here. ⊠ *Radisson Aruba Resort & Casino, J.E. Irausquin Blvd. 81, Palm Beach* ☎ *297/586–0096, 297/586–3900* ⊕ *www.uniquesportsaruba.com.*

WEST-SIDE DIVE SITES

Antilla **Wreck.** This German freighter, which sank off the northwest coast near Malmok Beach, is popular with both divers and snorkelers. Scuttled during World War II not long after its maiden voyage, the 400-foot-long vessel—referred to by locals as "the ghost ship"—has large compartments. You can climb into the captain's bathtub, which sits beside the wreck, for a unique photo op. Lobster, angelfish, yellowtail, and other fish swim about the wreck, which is blanketed by giant tube sponges and coral. ⊠ *Malmok Beach.*

Diving one of Aruba's many wrecks

Barcadera Reef. Only large types of coral—staghorn, elk-horn, pillar—find their niche close to this reef: the sand makes it difficult for the smaller varieties to survive. The huge (and abundant) sea fans here wave in the current.

Black Beach. The clear waters just off this beach are dotted with sea fans. The area takes its name from the rounded black stones lining the shore. It's the only bay on the island's north coast sheltered from thunderous waves, making it a safe spot for diving.

***Californian* Wreck.** Although this steamer is submerged at a depth that's perfect for underwater photography, this site is safe only for advanced divers; the currents here are strong, and the waters are dangerously choppy.

Harbour Reef. Steeply sloped boulders surrounded by a mul-titude of soft coral formations make this a great spot for novices. The calm waters are noteworthy for their abun-dance of fascinating plant life.

Malmok Reef. Lobsters and stingrays are among the high-lights at this bottom reef adorned by giant green, orange, and purple barrel sponges as well as leaf and brain coral. From here you can spot the *Debbie II,* a 120-foot barge that sank in 1992.

***Pedernales* Wreck.** During World War II this oil tanker was torpedoed by a German submarine. The U.S. military cut out the damaged centerpiece, towed the two remaining pieces to the States, and welded them together into a smaller vessel that eventually transported troops during the invasion of Normandy. The section that was left behind in shallow water is now surrounded by coral formations, making this a good site for novice divers. The ship's cabins, washbasins, and pipelines are exposed. The area teems with grouper and angelfish.

Skeleton Cave. Human bones found here (historians hypothesize that they're remains of ancient Arawak people) gave this dive spot its name. A large piece of broken rock forms the entrance where the cave meets the coast. ⊠ *Noord.*

Sonesta Reef. Two downed planes are the centerpiece of this interesting dive site near Sonesta Island. Several types of brain coral abound in this sandy-bottom area.

Tugboat Wreck. Spotted eagle rays and stingrays are sometimes observed at this shipwreck at the foot of Harbour Reef, which is one of Aruba's most popular. Spectacular formations of brain, sheet, and star coral blanket the path to the wreck, which is inhabited by several bright-green moray eels.

EAST-SIDE DIVE SITES

Captain Roger **Wreck.** A plethora of colorful fish swish about this old tugboat, which rests off the coast at Seroe Colorado. From shore you can swim to a steep coral reef.

De Palm Island. Secluded behind clusters of mangrove, the reef system around De Palm Island stretches all the way to Oranjestad. You can get close enough to touch the nurse sharks that sleep tucked into reef crevices during the day. ⊠ *De Palm Island.*

Isla di Oro. A wide expanse of reef grows far out along the shallow bank, making for superb diving. You'll be treated to views of green moray eels; coral crabs; trumpet fish; and French, gray, and queen angelfish.

Jane **Wreck.** This 200-foot freighter, lodged in an almost vertical position at a depth of 90 feet, is near the coral reef west of De Palm Island. Night diving is exciting here, as the polyps emerge from the corals that grow profusely on the steel plates of the decks and cabins. Soft corals and sea fans are also abundant in the area. ⊠ *De Palm Island.*

Punta Basora. This narrow reef stretches far into the sea off the island's easternmost point. On calm days you'll see eagle rays, stingrays, barracudas, and hammerhead sharks, as well as hawksbill and loggerhead turtles.

Shark Caves. At this site along the island's southeastern point you can swim alongside sand sharks and float past the nurse sharks sleeping under the rock outcroppings.

Vera Wreck. In 1954 this freighter sank while en route to North America. The crew, saved by an Aruban captain, claimed the ship held Nazi treasures.

The Wall. From May to August, green sea turtles intent on laying their eggs abound at this steep-walled reef. You'll also spot groupers and burrfish swimming nearby. Close to shore, massive sheet corals are plentiful; in the upper part of the reef are colorful varieties such as black coral, star coral, and flower coral. Flitting about are brilliant damselfish, rock beauties, and porgies.

SPECTATOR SPORTS

FAMILY **Compleho Deportivo Guillermo Prospero Trinidad.** You probably won't find Arubans singing "Take Me Out to the Ball Game," but come soccer season (late May–November, with matches on Tuesday, Thursday, Saturday, and Sunday) or at track-and-field meets, some 3,200 spirited fans pack into this complex. Events open with the Aruban national anthem, a display of flags, and the introduction of any old-timers in the stadium. Adult admission ranges from $3 to $6, depending on whether it's a local or international competition; children get in for just over a dollar. Regardless of what's on, you can hit the snack bar for such Aruban favorites as *pastechi* (meat-, cheese-, or seafood-filled turnovers) and *bitterballen* (bite-size meatballs), which you can wash down with a soda or a local Balashi beer. ✉ *Stadionweg, Oranjestad* ☎ *297/582–9550*.

SUBMARINE EXCURSIONS

Atlantis Submarines. Explore an underwater reef teeming with marine life without getting wet. Atlantis operates a 65-foot air-conditioned sub, *Atlantis VI*, which takes 48 passengers for a two-hour tour 95 to 150 feet below the surface along Barcadera Reef ($118 per person). There is no restroom on board, so plan accordingly. The company also owns the *Seaworld Explorer*, a semisubmersible that allows you to sit and view Aruba's marine habitat from 5 feet below the surface ($46 per person). Make reservations a day in advance. ⊠ *Renaissance Marina, L.G. Smith Blvd. 82, Oranjestad* ☎ *297/583–6090* ⊕ *www.depalmtours.com.*

TENNIS

Aruba Racquet Club. Aruba's winds make tennis a challenge even if you have the best of backhands. Although visitors can make arrangements to play at the resorts, priority goes to guests. Some private tennis clubs can also accommodate you. Or you can try the facilities at the Aruba Racquet Club. Host to a variety of international tournaments, the club has eight courts (six lighted), as well as a swimming pool, an aerobics center, and a restaurant. Fees are $15 per hour; a lesson with a pro costs $30 for a half hour, $50 for one hour. ⊠ *Rooisanto 21, Palm Beach* ☎ *297/586–0215* ⊕ *www.arc.aw.*

WINDSURFING

Aruba has all it takes for windsurfing: trade winds that average 15 knots year-round (peaking May–July), a sunny climate, and perfect azure-blue waters. With a few lessons from a certified instructor, even novices will be jibing in no time. The southwestern coast's tranquil waters make it ideal for both beginners and intermediates, as the winds are steady but sudden gusts rare. Experts will find the waters of the Atlantic, especially around Grapefield and Boca Grandi beaches, more challenging; winds are fierce and often shift without warning. Rentals average about $60 a day, and lessons range from $50 to $125. Many hotels include windsurfing in their watersports packages, and most operators can help you arrange complete windsurfing vacations.

Every June sees the Hi-Winds Pro-Am Windsurfing Competition, attracting professionals and amateurs from around the world. There are divisions for women, men, juniors, masters, and grand masters. Disciplines include slalom, course racing, long distance, and freestyle.

Aruba Beach Villas. You'll get first-rate instruction at Aruba Beach Villas. It's at Windsurf Village, a lodging complex created by and for windsurfers near Fisherman's Huts, a world-renowned sailing spot. The complex is also home to one of the Caribbean's largest and best-stocked windsurfing shops. ⊠ *L.G. Smith Blvd. 462, Malmok Beach* ☎ *297/586–2527, 800/320–9998 in U.S.* ⊕ *www.sailboard-vacations.com.*

DID YOU KNOW?

Near-constant trade winds that average 15 knots have made Aruba a popular wind-surfing destination, especially Grapefield, Boca Grandi, Malmok, and Fisherman's Huts beaches.

Sailboard Vacations. Complete windsurfing packages, including accommodations, can be arranged with Sailboard Vacations. Equipment can be rented for $60 a day. ⊠ *L.G. Smith Blvd. 462, Malmok Beach* ☎ *297/586–2527* ⊕ *www.sailboardvacations.com.*

Vela Aruba. This is the place to meet other windsurfers in town. It's a major kitesurfing center as well. ⊠ *L.G. Smith Blvd. 101, in front of the Marriott, Palm Beach* ☎ *297/586–3735* ⊕ *www.velawindsurf.com.*

SHOPS AND SPAS

SHOPPING CAN BE GOOD on Aruba. Although stores on the island often use the tagline "duty-free," the word "prices" is usually printed underneath in much smaller letters. Cheaper rents, lower taxes, and a willingness to add smaller markups mean that Aruban prices on many luxury goods are often reasonable, but not truly duty-free. Most North Americans, who find clothing to be less expensive back home, buy perfume and jewelry; South Americans tend to shell out lots of cash on a variety of brand-name merchandise.

Aruba's souvenir and crafts stores are full of Dutch porcelains and figurines, as befits the island's heritage. Dutch cheese is a good buy (you're allowed to bring up to 10 pounds of hard cheese through U.S. customs), as are hand-embroidered linens and any products made from the native aloe vera plant—sunburn cream, face masks, skin refreshers. Local arts and crafts run toward wood carvings and earthenware emblazoned with "Aruba: One Happy Island" and the like.

Island merchants are honest and pleasant. Still, if you encounter price markups, unsatisfactory service, or other shopping obstacles, call the tourist office, which will in turn contact the Aruba Merchants Association. A representative of the association will speak with the merchant on your behalf, even if the store isn't an association member.

When the stresses of sun and surf prove too much there's no shortage of spas to choose from on Aruba. The best spas are within the big resorts, particularly in the Palm Beach area. They offer a similar range of massage options, but relaxation treatments and amenities vary from one facility to the next. The legendary healing properties of the locally grown aloe plant are also available for those seeking a uniquely Aruban experience. When the intensity of the sun proves too much, several spas also offer cooling and relaxing post-burn treatments. In-room and couples treatments are widely available at larger resorts.

HOW AND WHEN

It's easy to spend money in Aruba. Most stores accept American currency and Aruban florins (written as "Afl") as well as credit cards and traveler's checks. Aruba has a 3% sales tax on most goods and services, which includes most purchases by tourists. Though many stores downtown advertise "duty-free" prices, Aruba isn't a duty-free port, so the only duty-free prices are to be had at the airport.

Good bargains are to be had for those who have a good knowledge of U.S. prices and who shop carefully. Don't try to bargain in stores, where it's considered rude to haggle. At flea markets and souvenir stands, however, you might be able to strike a deal.

Stores are open Monday through Saturday from 8:30 or 9 to 6. Some stores stay open through the lunch hour (noon to 2), and many open when cruise ships are in port on Sunday and holidays. The later you shop in downtown Oranjestad, the easier it will be to find a place to park. Also, later hours mean slightly lower temperatures. In fact, the Aruba Merchants Association is one force behind the effort to have shops stay open later, so that visitors who like to spend the day on the beach can shop in the cool of the evening.

ORANJESTAD AND ENVIRONS

MALLS AND MARKETPLACES

Caya G.F. Betico Croes. Aruba's chief shopping street, Caya G.F. Betico Croes is a busy thoroughfare and is lined with several shops advertising "duty-free prices" (again, these are not truly duty-free), boutiques, and jewelry stores noted for the aggressiveness of their vendors on cruise-ship days. ⊠ *Oranjestad.*

Dutch Crown Center. This tiny shopping center sandwiched between the major malls is easy to miss, but you shouldn't. You can find good swimwear and jewelry inside. ⊠ *L.G. Smith Blvd. 150 (some shops face Havenstraat), Oranjestad.*

Holland Aruba Mall. You'll find a collection of stylish shops such as Kenneth Cole and Perfume Palace, several souvenir shops and decent eateries including an outdoor café here. ⊠ *Havenstraat 6, Oranjestad.*

Port of Call Marketplace. Stores here sell fine jewelry, perfumes, low-priced liquor, batiks, crystal, leather goods, and fashionable clothing. ⊠ *L.G. Smith Blvd. 17, Oranjestad.*

Renaissance Mall. The upscale stores here, which include Guess, Lacoste, and Calvin Klein, have prices that are about the same as or more than in the U.S. ⊠ *Renaissance Hotel, L.G. Smith Blvd. 82, Oranjestad.*

9

Renaissance Marketplace (*Seaport Mall*). Five minutes from the cruise-ship terminal, the Renaissance Marketplace has more than 120 stores selling a variety of merchandise; the Seaport Casino is also here. ✉ *L.G. Smith Blvd. 9, Oranjestad.*

Royal Plaza Mall. Across from the cruise-ship terminal, the Royal Plaza Mall's pink, gabled building has cafés, a post office (open weekdays 8 to 3:30), and such stores as Nautica, Benetton, and Tommy Hilfiger. There's also a cyber-café. ✉ *L.G. Smith Blvd. 94, Oranjestad.*

Strada I and Strada II. These pastel-colored shopping complexes are in Dutch-style buildings. There are a variety of clothing shops including the ubiquitous Benetton and a branch of the phone company SETAR. ✉ *Klipstraat and Rifstraat, Oranjestad.*

SPECIALTY STORES

CIGARS

Cigar Emporium. The Cubans come straight from the climate-controlled humidor at Cigar Emporium. Choose from Cohiba, Montecristo, Romeo y Julieta, Partagas, and more. ✉ *Renaissance Mall, L.G. Smith Blvd. 82, Oranjestad* ☎ *297/582–5479.*

La Casa Del Habano. Fine cigars are sold here. ✉ *Royal Plaza Mall, L.G. Smith Blvd. 94, Oranjestad* ☎ *297/583–8509.*

Superior Tobacco. A good place to shop for stogies. ✉ *L.G. Smith Blvd. 120, Oranjestad* ☎ *297/582–3220.*

CLOTHING

Caperucita Raja. People come to Caperucita Raja for designer baby, children's, and junior clothes, as well as a wide selection of shoes. ✉ *Wilhelminastraat 17, Oranjestad* ☎ *297/583–6166.*

Colombia Moda. The lingerie sold here is made of high-quality microfiber fabrics. ✉ *Wilhelminastraat 19, Oranjestad* ☎ *297/582–3460.*

Del Sol. This is the place to buy beach accessories such as sun visors, and shirts and shorts that change colors in the sun. ✉ *Royal Plaza Mall, L.G. Smith Blvd. 94, Oranjestad* ☎ *297/583–8448.*

CLOSE UP

Ronchi de Cuba's Aruban Style

"Shopping has recently become tremendously advanced on Aruba," says local fashion designer Ronchi de Cuba. "We're seeing higher-end fashion that's more reasonably priced, from companies like Fendi and Gucci, and the shopping area is still growing." He says the best time to get great buys at the high-end stores is in January, when the holidays are over and the racks are being cleared for the new season.

De Cuba became involved in fashion at age 17, thanks to a high-school physical-education assignment for which he taught a dance class and presented a show that incorporated theater, choreography, and fashion. After attending college in Miami, de Cuba returned to his native Aruba to work at a modeling agency. Soon after, he opened his own agency to promote local entertainment and style.

The first Ronchi de Cuba design was a haute-couture number created for Miss Aruba 1999; he's since gone on to create ready-to-wear swimwear, menswear, women's wear, and junior lines. When he's not cutting clothes, the designer travels to New York, Miami, and Paris to peek into the shops and showrooms of major designers.

De Cuba clothes are constructed of fabrics suitable for a warm climate: crêpe linens, silk georgettes, and shantungs for day; brocade, wool crêpe, crêpe de Chine, and silk chiffon for evening. Inspired by such designers as John Galliano, Dolce & Gabbana, and Prada, his collections feature playful color schemes that incorporate dark solids, bright colors, and prints. He turns out a spring-summer collection and a holiday-cruise collection each year.

Always on the cutting edge of fashion, de Cuba is also known on the island for hosting the annual International Male Model contest, featuring dozens of contestants from the Caribbean, South and Central America, the United States, the United Arab Emirates, and Europe.

Look for de Cuba's label at stores in the Seaport Village Mall and the Royal Plaza Mall or at his own shop— Revolution—in Oranjestad.

9

Extreme Sports. Invest in a set of in-line skates or a boogie board, or pick up a backpack, bathing suit, or pair of reef walkers in funky shades at this hip sports shop. ⊠*Royal Plaza Mall, L.G. Smith Blvd. 94, Oranjestad* ☎*297/583–7105.*

La Venezolana. Menswear reigns supreme here. You can find blazers and suits as well as jeans, belts, and shoes. Look for such names as Givenchy, Lee Jeans, and Van Heusen. ✉ *Steenweg 12, Oranjestad* ☎ *297/582–1444.*

Mango. At this international chain, you can find fashions from as far away as Spain. ✉ *Caya Betico Croes 9, Oranjestad* ☎ *297/582–9700.*

Sun + Sand. As its many repeat customers will tell you, this is a great place for T-shirts, sweatshirts, polo shirts, and cover-ups. ✉ *Dutch Crown Center, L.G. Smith Blvd. 150, Oranjestad* ☎ *297/582–9700.*

Tommy Hilfiger. The activewear sold at Tommy Hilfiger makes it a great stop for a vacation wardrobe. A Tommy Jeans store is also here. ✉ *Royal Plaza Mall, L.G. Smith Blvd. 94, Oranjestad* ☎ *297/583–8548.*

★ Fodor'sChoice **Wulfsen & Wulfsen.** One of the most highly regarded clothing stores in Aruba and the Netherlands Antilles, Wulfsen & Wulfsen carries elegant suits for men and linen cocktail dresses for women. It's also a great place to buy Bermuda shorts. ✉ *Caya G.F. Betico Croes 52, Oranjestad* ☎ *297/582–3823.*

GIFTS AND SOUVENIRS

Creative Hands. There's an interesting selection of porcelain and ceramic miniatures of *cunucu* (country) houses and divi-divi trees, but the store's real draw is its exquisite Japanese dolls. ✉ *Socotorolaan 5, Oranjestad* ☎ *297/583–5665.*

El Bohio. You'll be charmed by El Bohio's wooden-hut displays holding Arawak-style pottery, Dutch shoes, and wind chimes. You can also find classic leather handbags. ✉ *Port of Call Marketplace, L.G. Smith Blvd. 17, Oranjestad* ☎ *297/582–9178.*

Kwa Kwa. Pottery lovers should head directly to the ceramic wind chimes, pottery, and knickknacks galore here. Other items include embroidered bags. ✉ *Port of Call Marketplace, L.G. Smith Blvd. 17, Oranjestad* ☎ *297/583–9471.*

★ Fodor'sChoice **The Mask.** Come here for intriguing souvenirs. Buds from the *mopa mopa* tree are boiled to form a resin, which is colored using vegetable dyes, then stretched by hand and mouth. Tiny pieces are cut and layered to form intricate designs—these are truly unusual gifts. ✉ *Paseo Herencia, J.E. Irausquin Blvd. 382A, Local C017, Palm Beach* ☎ *297/596–2900.*

Small, owner-operated souvenir shops abound in Aruba.

Tropical Wave. Clothes from Aruba and Indonesia, hand-painted mobiles, and bamboo wind chimes are among the goodies at Tropical Wave. ⊠ *Port of Call Marketplace, L.G. Smith Blvd. 17, Oranjestad* ☎ *297/582–1905.*

Vibes. Treat yourself to a Montecristo or Cohiba cigar, and pick up souvenirs such as postcards, picture frames, and T-shirts. ⊠ *Royal Plaza Mall, L.G. Smith Blvd. 93, Oranjestad* ☎ *297/583–7949.*

FOOD

Kong Hing Supermarket. This clean, orderly supermarket stocks all the comforts of home, including fresh cuts of meat, prepackaged salads, and a wide selection of beer, wine, and liquor. The market accepts credit cards for purchases of $10 or more, and there's also an ATM on the premises. ⊠ *L.G. Smith Blvd. 152, Bushiri* ☎ *297/582–5545* ☉ *Mon.–Sat. 8–8, Sun. 9–1.*

HOUSEWARES

Decor Home Fashions. Locals swear by this place, which sells sheets, towels, place mats, and other linens imported from Italy, Germany, Holland, Portugal, and the United States. ⊠ *Steenweg 14, Oranjestad* ☎ *297/582–6620.*

JEWELRY

Boolchand's. Boolchand's sells a wide variety of cameras including Olympus, GoPro, and Sony as well as electronics ranging from iPads to unlocked mobile phones. ⊠ *The Jewelry Centre, L.G. Smith Blvd. 90–92, Oranjestad* ☎ *297/582–9544.*

Colombian Emeralds. If green fire is your passion, Colombian Emeralds has a dazzling array. There are also fine European watches. ⊠ *Renaissance Mall, L.G. Smith Blvd. 82, Oranjestad* ☎ *297/583–6238.*

Diamonds International. For all that glitters, head to Diamonds International. ⊠ *Port of Call Marketplace, L.G. Smith Blvd. 17, Oranjestad* ☎ *800/515–3935* ⊕ *www.diamondsinternational.com.*

Gandelman Jewelers. This store sells Gucci and Rolex watches at reasonable prices, as well as gold bracelets and a full line of Lladro figurines. ⊠ *Renaissance Mall, Oranjestad* ☎ *297/583–4433.*

Grace Silver & Beyond. Come here for one-of-a-kind silver pieces. ⊠ *Seaport Marketplace 13, L.G. Smith Blvd. 9, Oranjestad* ☎ *297/588–6262.*

Pearl Gems Fine Jewelry. Precious pearls add luster to many of the pretty items at Pearl Gems. ⊠ *L.G. Smith Blvd. 90–92, Oranjestad* ☎ *297/588–4927.*

LEATHER GOODS

Alivio. Whether you're seeking something for just walking around town or for dressing up for dinner, you can find the right shoe in this Oranjestad shop. Look for Birkenstock from Germany, Piedro and Wolky from Holland, and Mephisto from France. Men's, women's, and children's shoes are all available. ⊠ *Steenweg 12-1, Oranjestad.*

Gucci. If you get lucky, you can catch one of the year's big sales (one is held the first week in December, the other the first week in February) at Gucci, when prices are slashed on handbags, luggage, wallets, shoes, watches, belts, and ties. ⊠ *Renaissance Mall, L.G. Smith Blvd. 82, Oranjestad* ☎ *297/583–3952.*

9

Beyond T-Shirts and Key Chains

You can't go wrong with baseball caps, refrigerator magnets, beer mugs, sweatshirts, T-shirts, key chains, and other local logo merchandise. You won't go broke buying these items, either.

Budget for a major purchase. If souvenirs are all about keeping the memories alive in the long haul, plan ahead to shop for something really special—a work of art, a rug or something else handcrafted, or a major accessory for your home. One major purchase will stay with you far longer than a dozen tourist trinkets.

Add to your collection. Whether antiques, used books, salt-and-pepper shakers, or ceramic frogs are your thing, start looking in the first day or two. Chances are you'll want to scout around and then go back to some of the first shops you visited before you hand over your credit card.

Get guarantees in writing. Is the vendor making promises? Ask him to put them in writing.

Anticipate a shopping spree. Pack a large tote bag in your suitcase in case you need extra space. If you think you might buy breakables, include a length of bubble wrap. Don't fill your suitcase to bursting before you leave home. Or include some old clothing that you can leave behind to make room for new acquisitions.

Know before you go. Study prices at home on items you might consider buying while you're away. Otherwise you won't recognize a bargain when you see one.

Plastic, please. Especially if your purchase is pricey and you're looking for authenticity, it's always smart to pay with a credit card. If a problem arises later and the merchant can't or won't resolve it, the credit-card company may help you out.

LUXURY GOODS

Aruba Trading Company. For perfumes, cosmetics, men's and women's clothing, and leather goods (including Bally shoes), stop in at Aruba Trading Company, which has been in business since the 1930s. ⊠ *Caya G.F. Betico Croes 12, Oranjestad* ☎ *297/582–2602.*

Little Switzerland. This Caribbean retail giant is the place to go for brand-name men's and women's fragrances, as well as china, crystal, and fine tableware. ⊠ *Royal Plaza Mall, L.G. Smith Blvd. 94, Oranjestad* ☎ *297/583– 4057* ⊠ *Westin Resort, J.E. Irausquin Blvd, Palm Beach* ☎ *248/809–5560.*

Weitnauer. You can find specialty Lenox items as well as a wide range of fragrances here. ✉ *Caya G.F. Betico Croes 29, Oranjestad* ☎ *297/582–2790.*

PERFUMES

Aruba Trading Company, Little Switzerland, and Weitnauer are also known for their extensive fragrance offerings (⇨ *see Luxury Goods, above*).

J.L. Penha & Sons. A venerated name in Aruba, J.L. Penha sells high-end perfumes and cosmetics. It stocks such brands as Boucheron, Cartier, Dior, and Givenchy. ✉ *Caya G.F. Betico Croes 11/13, Oranjestad* ☎ *297/582–4160, 297/582–4161.*

MANCHEBO AND DRUIF BEACHES

GIFTS AND SOUVENIRS

Alhambra Casino Shopping Arcade. Souvenir shops, boutiques, and fast-food outlets fill the arcade, which is open until midnight. It's attached to the popular casino. ✉ *L.G. Smith Blvd. 47, Manchebo Beach.*

EAGLE BEACH

FOOD

Ling & Sons Supermarket. The family-owned-and-operated supermarket is one of the island's top grocers. In addition to a wide variety of foods, there's a bakery, a deli, a butcher shop, and a well-stocked "liquortique." If you email ahead, the store can have a package of groceries delivered to your hotel room. The market is open Monday to Saturday 8 to 8 and Sunday 9 to 1. Before the December holidays, the store sometimes stays open an hour later on weekdays. ✉ *Italiëstraat 26, Eagle Beach* ☎ *297/583–2370* ⊕ *www.lingandsons.com.*

SPAS

Intermezzo Spa. This full-service spa offers a range of treatments at some of the best prices on the island—almost all 60-minute treatments are under $100. Earth tones and a vaguely Asian feel set the stage for pure relaxation. The aromatherapy, deep-tissue, and acupressure massages are especially popular. In cases where couples can't be accom-

modated because of space or staffing limitations, a shuttle
will whisk them off to the spa's branch at the ▢▢▢▢
Mill Resort. When the intense Aruba sun play▢
with delicate skin there's a "nourishing wrap,▢
promises to return suppleness and moisture usin▢
grown aloe and a custom blend of ingredients. ⊠ ▢
Tara Beach Resorts, L.G. Smith Blvd. 55B, Eag▢
☏*297/583–1100* ☞ *$85, 60-min massage. $260▢*
spa packages. Hair salon, hot tub. Gym with▢
vascular machines, free weights. Services: Arom▢
body wraps, facials, massage.

PALM BEACH AND NOORD

GIFTS AND SOUVENIRS

Artistic Boutique. This boutique is known for it▢
Armani figurines from Italy, usually sold at ▢
count; Aruban hand-embroidered linens; gol▢
jewelry; and porcelain and pottery from Sp▢
Smith Blvd. 90–92, Oranjestad ☏*297/588–246▢*
Inn Resort Aruba, J.E. Irausquin Blvd. 230, ▢
☏*297/583–3383.*

LEATHER GOODS

Ferragamo. This popular boutique carries ▢
designers shoes, handbags, and other access▢
Smith Blvd. 95, Palm Beach Plaza Mall, ▢
☏*297/596–2072.*

Mario Hernandez. This Colombian designer offers some spectacular examples of quality leatherwork in his handbags,
jackets, shoes, and accessories. ⊠*Paseo Herencia, L.G.
Smith Blvd. 382, Palm Beach* ☏*297/586–0300.*

MALLS

Paseo Herencia. It's all about style at this shopping center,
which is just minutes away from the high-rise hotel area.
The great bell tower, the nightly dancing-waters shows,
and the selection of restaurants pull in shoppers. Offerings
include Cuban cigars, the sportswear of Lacoste, Italian
denim goods at Moda & Stile, perfumes, cosmetics, and
lots of souvenir shops. ⊠*L.G. Smith Blvd., Palm Beach*
☏*297/586–6533.*

---

almost limitless list of pampering options. The rum-and-
aloe massage uses two of the island's most loved products
to create 80 minutes of pure bliss. All the usual massage
options are here as well as some unique offerings such as the
tiger clam–shell and mango massage. The "I Deserve It!"
package offers four hours of treatments and a delicious spa
lunch. ⊠ *Radisson Aruba Resort & Casino, J.E. Irausqu▢
Blvd. 81, Palm Beach* ☏*297/526–6053* ☞ *$125, 50–▢
massage. $352 half-day spa packages. Hair salon, hot▢
sauna, steam room. Gym with: Cardiovascular mac▢
free weights, weight-training equipment. Services:▢
therapy, body wraps, facials, hydrotherapy, massa▢
shower. Classes and programs: Aqua-aerobic▢
Pilates, spinning, yoga.*

Nafanny Spa. Massage therapist Fanny Lam▢
yard in Alto Vista provide a peaceful a▢
backdrop for the pure relaxation to com▢
bamboo, and hot-stone massages are▢
various treatments including a 90-m▢
session and numerous facial treatr▢
botanicals designed to ease away▢
lines. The location is a bit remote▢
makes that something of an adv▢
pick up clients at their resort.▢
offered. Though not offered▢
half- and full-day spa bund▢
Spa isn't the fanciest on▢
attention is unbeatable a▢
39F, Noord ☏*297/586–▢
50-min Swedish mass▢
wraps, facials, massa▢*

Okeanos. The ocea▢
in the Renaissanc▢
seems a world a▢
massages and ▢
of nature in▢
assortment▢
both anti-▢
a huge n▢
combin▢
own b▢
Ther▢
at ▢
⊠ ▢

Larimar S▢
Radisson o▢
ence on the isla▢
everything from hy▢

Weitnauer. You can find specialty Lenox items as well as a wide range of fragrances here. ⊠ *Caya G.F. Betico Croes 29, Oranjestad* ☏ *297/582–2790.*

PERFUMES

Aruba Trading Company, Little Switzerland, and Weitnauer are also known for their extensive fragrance offerings *(⇨ see Luxury Goods, above).*

J.L. Penha & Sons. A venerated name in Aruba, J.L. Penha sells high-end perfumes and cosmetics. It stocks such brands as Boucheron, Cartier, Dior, and Givenchy. ⊠ *Caya G.F. Betico Croes 11/13, Oranjestad* ☏ *297/582–4160, 297/582–4161.*

MANCHEBO AND DRUIF BEACHES

GIFTS AND SOUVENIRS

Alhambra Casino Shopping Arcade. Souvenir shops, boutiques, and fast-food outlets fill the arcade, which is open until midnight. It's attached to the popular casino. ⊠ *L.G. Smith Blvd. 47, Manchebo Beach.*

EAGLE BEACH

FOOD

Ling & Sons Supermarket. The family-owned-and-operated supermarket is one of the island's top grocers. In addition to a wide variety of foods, there's a bakery, a deli, a butcher shop, and a well-stocked "liquortique." If you email ahead, the store can have a package of groceries delivered to your hotel room. The market is open Monday to Saturday 8 to 8 and Sunday 9 to 1. Before the December holidays, the store sometimes stays open an hour later on weekdays. ⊠ *Italiëstraat 26, Eagle Beach* ☏ *297/583–2370* ⊕ *www. lingandsons.com.*

9

SPAS

Intermezzo Spa. This full-service spa offers a range of treatments at some of the best prices on the island—almost all 60-minute treatments are under $100. Earth tones and a vaguely Asian feel set the stage for pure relaxation. The aromatherapy, deep-tissue, and acupressure massages are especially popular. In cases where couples can't be accommodated because of space or staffing limitations, a shuttle will whisk them off to the spa's branch at the nearby Mill Resort. When the intense Aruba sun plays havoc with delicate skin there's a "nourishing wrap," which promises to return suppleness and moisture using locally grown aloe and a custom blend of ingredients. ✉ *Bucuti & Tara Beach Resorts, L.G. Smith Blvd. 55B, Eagle Beach* ☎ *297/583–1100* ☞ *$85, 60-min massage. $260 half-day spa packages. Hair salon, hot tub. Gym with: Cardiovascular machines, free weights. Services: Aromatherapy, body wraps, facials, massage.*

PALM BEACH AND NOORD

GIFTS AND SOUVENIRS

Artistic Boutique. This boutique is known for its Giuseppe Armani figurines from Italy, usually sold at a 20% discount; Aruban hand-embroidered linens; gold and silver jewelry; and porcelain and pottery from Spain. ✉ *L.G. Smith Blvd. 90–92, Oranjestad* ☎ *297/588-2468* ✉ *Holiday Inn Resort Aruba, J.E. Irausquin Blvd. 230, Palm Beach* ☎ *297/583–3383.*

LEATHER GOODS

Ferragamo. This popular boutique carries the famous designers shoes, handbags, and other accessories. ✉ *L.G. Smith Blvd. 95, Palm Beach Plaza Mall, Palm Beach* ☎ *297/596-2072.*

Mario Hernandez. This Colombian designer offers some spectacular examples of quality leatherwork in his handbags, jackets, shoes, and accessories. ✉ *Paseo Herencia, L.G. Smith Blvd. 382, Palm Beach* ☎ *297/586-0300.*

MALLS

Paseo Herencia. It's all about style at this shopping center, which is just minutes away from the high-rise hotel area. The great bell tower, the nightly dancing-waters shows, and the selection of restaurants pull in shoppers. Offerings include Cuban cigars, the sportswear of Lacoste, Italian denim goods at Moda & Stile, perfumes, cosmetics, and lots of souvenir shops. ✉ *L.G. Smith Blvd., Palm Beach* ☎ *297/586-6533.*

Many Aruba resorts have their own spas providing body treatments and massages.

PERFUMES

Maggy's. You'll find a nice selection of high-end perfumes and cosmetics here. There's also a full-service salon at both locations. ⊠ *Renaissance Mall, L.G. Smith Blvd. 9, Lot 3-B, Oranjestad* ☎ *297/583–6108* ⊕ *www.maggysaruba. aw* ⊗ *Mon.–Sat. 10–7, Sun. 10–2* ⊠ *Paseo Herencia, L.G. Smith Blvd. 382, Palm Beach* ☎ *297/586–2113.*

SPAS

Etnika Spa. This elegant getaway at the Westin makes a special effort to cater to couples looking to de-stress together. Within the calming confines guests can look forward to a range of treatments with an emphasis on marine treatments designed to rejuvenate and detoxify. Despite the serene surroundings and top-class amenities available in this oasis, many resort guests opt for the in-room treatments. ⊠ *Westin Aruba Resort & Casino, J.E. Irausquin Blvd. 77, Palm Beach* ☎ *297/586–4466* ☞ *$140, 50-min massage. $350 day-spa packages. Hair salon, hot tub, sauna, steam room. Services: Aromatherapy, body wraps, facials, hydrotherapy, massage.*

Larimar Spa and Salon. The expansive oceanfront spa at the Radisson offers possibly the most complete spa experience on the island. The bamboo and pastel interior has everything from hydrotherapy to a full workout and an almost limitless list of pampering options. The rum-and-aloe massage uses two of the island's most loved products to create 80 minutes of pure bliss. All the usual massage options are here as well as some unique offerings such as the tiger clam–shell and mango massage. The "I Deserve It!" package offers four hours of treatments and a delicious spa lunch. ⊠ *Radisson Aruba Resort & Casino, J.E. Irausquin Blvd. 81, Palm Beach* ☎*297/526–6053* ☞ *$125, 50-min massage. $352 half-day spa packages. Hair salon, hot tub, sauna, steam room. Gym with: Cardiovascular machines, free weights, weight-training equipment. Services: Aromatherapy, body wraps, facials, hydrotherapy, massage, Vichy shower. Classes and programs: Aqua-aerobics, cycling, Pilates, spinning, yoga.*

Nafanny Spa. Massage therapist Fanny Lampe's home and yard in Alto Vista provide a peaceful and picturesque backdrop for the pure relaxation to come. Thai, Swedish, bamboo, and hot-stone massages are all on offer as are various treatments including a 90-minute wine-therapy session and numerous facial treatments using soothing botanicals designed to ease away impurities and stress lines. The location is a bit remote but the tranquil setting makes that something of an advantage. Fanny will often pick up clients at their resort. Daily yoga classes are also offered. Though not offered as a package, customized half- and full-day spa bundles can be created. Nafanny Spa isn't the fanciest on the island, but the individual attention is unbeatable and so are the prices. ⊠ *Alto Vista 39F, Noord* ☎*297/586–3007* ⊕ *www.nafanny.com* ☞ *$70, 50-min Swedish massage. Services: Aromatherapy, body wraps, facials, massage, yoga.*

Okeanos. The ocean provides the backdrop for this spa in the Renaissance, which has its own massage cove that seems a world apart from the rest of the resort. Outdoor massages and showers help to bring the calming effects of nature into the treatments. In addition to the usual assortment of massages and wraps, the spa also offers both anti-cellulite and anti-aging treatments. There are a huge number of packages available including one that combines Swedish massage with a meal served by your own butler. Pampering doesn't get much better than this. There are also optional packages to use the spa services at the Cove Spa located on the resort's private island. ⊠ *Renaissance Aruba Resort & Casino, L.G. Smith Blvd. 82, Palm Beach* ☎*297/583–6000* ⊕ *www.renaissancearu-*

baspa.com ☞ *$140, 75-min massage. $525 day-spa packages. Hair salon, hot tub, sauna, steam room. Gym with: Cardiovascular machines, free weights, weight-training equipment. Services: Aromatherapy, body wraps, facials, hydrotherapy, massage.*

ZoiA Spa. It's all about indulgence at the Hyatt's upscale spa. Gentle music and the scent of botanicals make the world back home fade into the background. Newly arrived visitors to the island can opt for the jet lag massage that combines reflexology and aromatherapy, before getting into the swing of things. Those with the budget and time for a full day of relaxation can opt for the Serene package, and there's even a mother-to-be package available. Island brides can avail themselves of a full menu of beauty services ranging from botanical facials (using local ingredients) to a full makeup job for the big day. The Pure High Tea package offers a delicious assortment of snacks and teas along with an hour of treatments. ✉ *Hyatt Regency Aruba Beach Resort & Casino, J.E. Irausquin Blvd. 85, Palm Beach* ☎ *297/586–1234* ⊕ *www.aruba.hyatt.com* ☞ *$145, 60-min massage. $575 day-spa packages. Hair salon, hot tub, sauna, steam room. Services: Aromatherapy, body wraps, facials, hydrotherapy, massage.*

9

TRAVEL SMART
ARUBA

GETTING HERE AND AROUND

Aruba is a small island, so it's virtually impossible to get lost when exploring. Most activity takes place in and around Oranjestad or in the two main hotel areas, which are designated as the "low-rise" and "high-rise" areas. Main roads on the island are generally excellent, but getting to some of the more secluded beaches or historic sites will involve driving on unpaved tracks. Though Aruba is an arid island, there are periods of heavy rain, and it's best to avoid exploring the national park or other wilderness areas during these times, since roads can become flooded, and muddy conditions can make driving treacherous.

■TIP→ Ask the local tourist board about hotel and local transportation packages that include tickets to major museum exhibits or other special events.

▌ AIR TRAVEL

Aruba is 2½ hours from Miami, 4½ hours from New York, and 9½ hours from Amsterdam. The flight from New York to San Juan, Puerto Rico takes 3½ hours; from Miami to San Juan it's 1½ hours; and from San Juan to Aruba it's just over an hour. Shorter still is the ¼- to ½-hour hop (depending on whether you take a prop or a jet plane) from Curaçao to Aruba.

Airlines and Airports Airline and Airport Links.com. Airline and Airport Links.com has links to many of the world's airlines and airports. ⊕ *www.airlineandairportlinks.com.*

Airline-Security Issues Transportation Security Administration. The TSA has answers for almost every question that might come up. ⊕ *www.tsa.gov.*

AIRPORTS

Aruba's Aeropuerto Internacional Reina Beatrix (Queen Beatrix International Airport, AUA), near the island's south coast, is a modern, passenger-friendly facility.

Airport Information Aeropuerto Internacional Reina Beatrix ☎ *297/524–2424* ⊕ *www.airport aruba.com.*

GROUND TRANSPORTATION

A taxi from the airport to most hotels takes about 20 minutes. It'll cost $17 to get to the hotels along Eagle Beach, $20 to the high-rise hotels on Palm Beach, and $10 to the hotels downtown (rates are a few dollars higher at night). You'll find a taxi stand right outside the baggage-claim area.

FLIGHTS

There are nonstop flights to Aruba from Boston, Charlotte, Chicago (seasonal service), Houston, Miami, Newark, New York–JFK, and Philadelphia. Canadian travelers may fly nonstop during high travel season but must connect through the United States or Caracas, Venezuela at other times.

Checking in, paying departure taxes (if they aren't included in your ticket), clearing security, and boarding can take time on Aruba. Because security has gotten tighter, get to the airport at least three hours ahead of time. You may be randomly selected for inspection of your carry-on baggage at the gate. Regulations prohibit packing certain items in your carry-on luggage, including matches, lighters, and handheld radios. Check with your hotel concierge before packing to return home.

Airline Contacts Air Canada ☎ 888/247–2262 in North America ⊕ www.aircanada.com. **American Airlines** ☎ 297/582–2700 on Aruba, 800/433–7300 ⊕ www.aa.com. **Delta Airlines** ☎ 297/800–1555 on Aruba, 800/221–1212 for U.S. reservations, 800/241–4141 for international reservations ⊕ www. delta.com. **Dutch Antilles Express** ☎ 599/588–1900 ⊕ www.flydae.com. **jetBlue** ☎ 800/538–2583 ⊕ www. jetblue.com. **KLM** ☎ 5999/868–0195 on Aruba, ⊕ www.klm.com. **Spirit Airlines** ☎ 800/772–7117 ⊕ www.spiritair.com. **United Airlines** ☎ 297/562–9592 on Aruba, 800/538–2929 in North America ⊕ www.united.com. **US Airways** ☎ 800/428–4322 for U.S. and Canada reservations, 800/622–1015 for international reservations ⊕ www.usairways.com.

▌ BUS TRAVEL

Each day, from 6 am to midnight, buses make hourly trips between the beach hotels and downtown Oranjestad. The one-way fare is $1.25, and the round-trip fare is $2.25. Exact change is preferred. Buses also run down the coast from Oranjestad to San Nicolas for the same fare. Contact the Aruba Tourism Authority for schedules. Buses run from the airport terminal to hotels every 15 minutes during the day until 8 pm, and once an hour from 8:40 pm to 12:40 am.

▌ CAR TRAVEL

Most of Aruba's major attractions are fairly easy to find; others you'll happen upon only by sheer luck (or with an Aruban friend). International traffic signs and Dutch-style traffic signals (with an extra light for a turning lane) can be misleading if you're not used to them; use extreme caution, especially at intersections, until you grasp the rules of the road.

GASOLINE

Gas prices average a little more than $1.25 a liter (roughly a quarter of a gallon), which is reasonable by Caribbean standards. Stations are plentiful in and near Oranjestad, San Nicolas, and Santa Cruz, and near the major high-rise hotels on the western coast. All take cash, and most take major credit cards. Unlike in the U.S., gas prices aren't posted prominently, since they're fixed and the same at all stations.

PARKING

There aren't any parking meters in downtown Oranjestad, and finding an open spot is very difficult. Try the lot on Caya G.F. Betico Croes across from the First National Bank, the one on Havenstraat near the Chez Matilde restaurant, or the one on Emanstraat near the water tower. Rates average $1.25 an hour, but some charge almost twice that.

RENTAL CARS

In Aruba you must meet the minimum age requirements of each rental service (Budget, for example, requires drivers to be over 25; Avis, over 23; and Hertz, over 21). A signed credit-card slip or a cash deposit of $500 is required. Rates for unlimited mileage are between $35 and $65 a day, with local agencies generally offering lower rates. Insurance is available starting at about $10 per day. Try to make reservations before arriving, and opt for a four-wheel-drive vehicle if you plan to explore the island.

Contacts Avis ⊠ *Paseo Herencia Mall, Palm Beach* ☎ *297/587–7202, 800/522–9696* ⊕ *www.avis.com* ✉ *Airport* ☎ *297/587–7202.* **Budget** ⊠ *Camacuri 10, Oranjestad* ☎ *297/582–8600, 800/472–3325* ⊕ *www.budget.com.* **Economy** ⊠ *Bushiri 27, Oranjestad* ☎ *297/582–0009* ⊕ *www.economy aruba.com.* **Hertz** ⊠ *Sabana Blanco 35, near airport* ☎ *297/582–1845, 800/654–3001* ⊕ *www.hertz. com* ✉ *Airport* ☎ *297/588–7570.* **Thrifty** ⊠ *Wayaca 33-F, Oranjestad* ☎ *297/583–4042* ⊕ *www.thrifty.com* ✉ *Airport* ☎ *297/583–4902.*

RENTAL CAR INSURANCE

Everyone who rents a car wonders whether the insurance that the rental companies offer is worth the expense. No one—including us—has a simple answer. If you own a car, your personal auto insurance may cover a rental to some degree, though not all policies protect you abroad; always read your policy's fine print. If you don't have auto insurance, then seriously consider buying the collision- or loss-damage waiver (CDW or LDW) from the car-rental company, which eliminates your liability for damage to the car. Some credit cards offer CDW coverage, but it's usually supplemental to your own insurance and rarely covers SUVs, minivans, or luxury models. If your coverage is secondary, you may still be liable for loss-of-use costs from the car-rental company. But no credit-card insurance is valid unless you use that card for *all* transactions, from reserving to paying the final bill. It's sometimes cheaper to buy insurance as part of your general travel-insurance policy.

ROADSIDE EMERGENCIES

Discuss with the rental-car agency what to do in the case of an emergency. Make sure you understand what your insurance covers and what it doesn't; let someone at your accommodation know where you're heading and when you plan to return. If you find yourself stranded, hail a taxi or speak to the locals, who may have some helpful advice about finding your way to a phone or a bus stop. Keep emergency numbers with you, just in case. Because Aruba is such a small island, you should never panic if you have car trouble; it's likely you'll be within relatively easy walking distance of a populated area.

ROAD CONDITIONS

Aside from the major highways, the island's winding roads are poorly marked (although the situation is slowly improving). Keep an eye out for rocks and other debris when driving on remote roads.

RULES OF THE ROAD

Driving here is on the right side of the road, American-style. Despite the laid-back ways of locals, when they get behind the steering wheel they often speed and take liberties with road rules, especially outside the more heavily traveled Oranjestad and hotel areas. Keep a watchful eye for passing cars and for vehicles coming out of side roads. Speed limits are rarely posted, but the maximum speed is 60 kph (40 mph) and 40 kph (25 mph) through settlements. Speed limits and the use of seat belts are enforced.

▮ TAXI TRAVEL

There's a dispatch office at the airport; you can also flag down taxis on the street (look for license plates with a "TX" tag). Rates are fixed (i.e., there are no meters; the rates are set by the government and displayed on a chart), though you and the driver should agree on the fare before your ride begins. Add $2 to the fare after midnight and $2 to $4 on Sunday and holidays. An hour-long island tour costs about $40, with up to four people. Rides into town from Eagle Beach run about $10; from Palm Beach, about $11.

Contact **Airport Taxi Dispatch** ☎ *297/582–2116.*

ESSENTIALS

▮ ACCOMMODATIONS

In Aruba hotels usually add an 11% service charge to the bill and collect 8% in government taxes for a whopping total of 19% on top of quoted rates.

Most hotels and other lodgings require you to give your credit-card details before they'll confirm your reservation. If you don't feel comfortable emailing this information, ask if you can fax it (some places even prefer faxes). However you book, get confirmation in writing and have a copy of it handy when you check in.

Be sure you understand the hotel's cancellation policy. Some places allow you to cancel without any kind of penalty—even if you pre-paid to secure a discounted rate—if you cancel at least 24 hours in advance. Others require you to cancel a week in advance or penalize you the cost of one night. Small inns and B&Bs are most likely to require you to cancel far in advance. Most hotels allow children under a certain age to stay in their parents' room at no extra charge, but others charge for them as extra adults; find out the cutoff age for discounts.

▬TIP→ Hotels have private bathrooms, phones, and TVs, and don't offer meals unless we specify a meal plan in the review (i.e., breakfast, some meals, all meals, all-inclusive). We always list facilities but not whether you'll be charged an extra fee to use them.

For lodging price categories, consult the price chart at the beginning of the Where to Stay chapter.

APARTMENT AND HOUSE RENTALS

Apartments and time-share condos are common in Aruba. So if you're looking for more space for your family or group to spread out in (and especially if you want to have access to a kitchen to make some meals), this can be a very budget-friendly option in Aruba. The money you save can be used for more dining and activities. Many time-share resorts are full-service, offering the same range of watersports and other activities as any other resort. And some regular resorts also have a time-share component.

Contacts Forgetaway
⊕ *www.forgetaway.com.*
Home Away ☎ *512/493–0382*
in U.S. ⊕ *www.homeaway.com.*
Villas International ☎ *415/499–9490, 800/221–2260 in U.S.*
⊕ *www.villasintl.com.*

HOTELS

Aruba is a major tourist destination and offers a variety of hotel types. Most hotels are located in one of two stretches: the low-rise hotels in a stretch along Druif Beach and Eagle Beach, and the high-rise hotels on a stretch of Palm Beach. With a few exceptions, the hotels in the high-rise area tend to be larger and more expensive than their low-rise counterparts, but they usually offer a wider range of services.

ADDRESSES

"Informal" might best describe Aruban addresses. Sometimes the street designation is in English (as in J.E. Irausquin Boulevard), other times in Dutch (as in Wilhelminastraat); sometimes it's not specified whether something is a boulevard or a *straat* (street) at all. Street numbers follow street names, and postal codes aren't used. In rural areas you might have to ask a local for directions—and be prepared for such instructions as "Take a right at the market, then a left where you see the big dividivi tree."

COMMUNICATIONS

INTERNET
Most hotels now have some kind of Internet connection. In Oranjestad, Internet Planet is the place to check your email. It's in the Renaissance Mall.

Contacts Cybercafes
⊕ *www.cybercafes.com.*

PHONES
To call Aruba direct from the United States, dial 011–297, followed by the seven-digit number in Aruba. International, direct, and operator-assisted calls from Aruba to all countries in the world are possible via hotel operators or from the Government Long Distance Telephone, Telegraph, and Radio Office (SETAR), in the

HOTEL TIPS

Remember the taxes. Taxes and service charges add up to 19% to your hotel bill.

Avoid peak season (November through April). Rates often double in peak season, and the beaches are also more crowded.

Book in advance. Many hotels and attractions offer Internet-only specials that can mean a savings of more than 10%.

Consider a room without an ocean view. There can be a huge price difference between a room with a view and one with no view.

Do you really need all-inclusive? Although AI resorts might seem to be a better bargain, they limit your dining and nightlife options.

Consider your options. There are many large luxury resorts, but smaller resorts are cheaper, less crowded, and offer more personal service.

Not sure where to stay? Aruba Tourism Authority has a comprehensive list of accommodations (⊕ *www.aruba.com*), and staff members are always ready to help find accommodations to suit any budget.

post-office building in Oranjestad. When making calls on Aruba, simply dial the seven-digit number. AT&T customers can dial 800–8000 from special phones at the cruise dock and in the airport's arrival and departure halls and charge calls to their credit card. From other phones, dial 121 to contact the SETAR international operator to place a collect or AT&T calling-card call. Local calls from pay phones, which accept both local currency and phone cards, cost 25¢. Business travelers or vacationers who need to be in regular contact with their families at home can rent an international cell phone from the concierge in most hotels or at some local electronics stores.

LOCAL CALLS
Dial the seven-digit number.

CALLING THE U.S.
Dial 0, then 1, the area code, and the number.

CALLING CARDS
The cheapest way to phone home is by using a phone card to dial direct. You can buy phone cards at SETAR offices, newsagents, supermarkets, and some pharmacies and gas stations.

MOBILE PHONES
Aruba has excellent cellular coverage, and there are only a few remote spots where coverage is spotty. Both SETAR and Digicel offer rental phones, but take note of the cost, as the rental charges and deposit may make purchasing a cheap phone a better choice, especially if you're staying more

FODORS.COM

Before your trip, be sure to check out what other travelers are saying in Talk on www.fodors.com.

than a week. Most U.S.–based GSM and CDMA cell phones work on Aruba.

If you have a multiband phone (some countries use frequencies different from those used in the United States) and your service provider uses the world-standard GSM network (as do T-Mobile, Cingular, and Verizon), you can probably use your phone abroad. Roaming fees can be steep. And overseas you normally pay the toll charges for incoming calls. It's almost always cheaper to send a text message than to make a call.

If you just want to make local calls, consider buying a new SIM card (note that your provider may have to unlock your phone for you to use a different SIM card) and a prepaid service plan in the destination. You'll then have a local number and can make local calls at local rates. If your trip is extensive, you could also simply buy a new cell phone in your destination, as the initial cost will be offset over time.

■TIP→ If you travel internationally frequently, save one of your old mobile phones or buy a cheap one on the Internet; ask your cell-phone company to unlock it for you, and take it with you as a travel phone, buying a new SIM card with pay-as-you-go service in each destination.

Contacts **Aruba Cellular**
☎ *297/563–1500* ⊕ *www.aruba
cellular.com.* **Aruba Discount
Cell** ☎ *297/732–8809* ⊕ *www.
arubadiscountcell.com.* **Digicel**
☎ *297/522–2222* ⊕ *www.digicel
aruba.com.* **SETAR** ☎ *297/525–1000*
⊕ *www.setar.aw.*

▌ CUSTOMS AND DUTIES

You can bring up to 1 liter of spirits, 3 liters of beer, or 2.25 liters of wine per person, and up to 200 cigarettes or 50 cigars into Aruba. You don't need to declare the value of gifts or other items, although customs officials may inquire about large items or large quantities of goods and charge (at their discretion) an import tax of 7.5% to 22% on items worth more than $230. Meat, birds, and illegal substances are forbidden. You may be asked to provide written verification that plants are free of diseases. If you're traveling with pets, bring a veterinarian's note attesting to their good health.

Aruba Information Aruba Customs Office ☎ *297/582–1800.*

U.S. Information U.S. Customs and Border Protection
⊕ *www.cbp.gov.*

▌ EATING OUT

Unless otherwise noted, the restaurants listed in this guide are open daily for lunch and dinner.

Aruba offers a startling variety of eating options thanks to the tourist trade, with choices ranging from upscale to simple roadside dining. The island is also a particularly family-friendly destination, so bringing the kids along is rarely a problem, and many restaurants offer children's menus. Arubans love their meat, as shown by the ubiquity of steak joints, so vegetarians may be left feeling that everyone on the island is a carnivore; however, most kitchens are able to create a special vegetarian meal upon request if there's no vegetarian option listed on the menu.

CELL PHONE TIPS

You can purchase a cheap cell phone at numerous outlets and simply "top-up" (pay as you go). Incoming calls are free, so have your family call you to save on exorbitant island rates and huge roaming charges. Not all cell phones from home will work in Aruba (some do, but you never know which ones until you're actually on-island), even if the phone company tells you it does.

ARUBAN CUISINE

Aruba shares many of its traditional foods with Bonaire and Curaçao. These dishes are a fusion of the various influences that have shaped the culture of the islands. Proximity to mainland South America means that many traditional snack and breakfast foods of Venezuelan origin, such as *empanadas* (a fried cornmeal dumpling filled with ground meat), are widely found. The Dutch influence is evident in the fondness for cheese of all sorts, but especially Gouda. *Keshi yena,* ground meat with seasonings and wrapped in cheese before baking, is a national obsession.

If there's one thread that unites the cuisines of the Caribbean it's cornmeal, and Arubans love nothing more than a side of *funchi* (like a thick polenta) or a *pan bati* (a fried cornmeal pancake) to make a traditional meal complete. Though Aruban cuisine isn't by nature spicy, it's almost always accompanied by a small bowl of spicy *pika* (a condiment of fiery hot peppers and onions in vinegar). An abundance of seafood means that seafood is the most popular protein on the island, and it's been said that if there were an Aruban national dish it would be the catch of the day.

PAYING

We assume that restaurants and hotels accept credit cards. If they don't, we'll note it in the review.

For guidelines on tipping see Tipping, below.

RESERVATIONS AND DRESS

We only mention reservations when they're essential (there's no other way you'll ever get a table) or when they're not accepted. We mention dress only when men are required to wear a jacket or a jacket and tie.

WINES, BEER, AND SPIRITS

Arubans have a great love for wine, so even small supermarkets have a fairly good selection of European and South American wines at prices that are reasonable by Caribbean standards. The beer

WORD OF MOUTH

Was the service stellar or not up to snuff? Did the food give you shivers of delight or leave you cold? Did the prices and portions make you happy or sad? Rate restaurants and write your own reviews in Travel Ratings or start a discussion about your favorite places in Travel Talk on www.fodors.com. Your comments might even appear in our books. Yes, you, too, can be a correspondent!

of choice in Aruba is the island-brewed Balashi, though many also favor the deliciously crisp Amstel Bright, which is brewed on nearby Curaçao.

▮ ELECTRICITY

Aruba runs on a 110-volt cycle, the same as in the United States; outlets are usually the two-prong variety. Total blackouts are rare, and most large hotels have backup generators.

▮ EMERGENCIES

The number to call in case of emergency—911—is the same as in the U.S.

▮ HEALTH

As a rule, water is pure and food is wholesome in hotels and local restaurants throughout Aruba, but be cautious when buying food from street vendors. And just as you would at home, wash or peel all fruits and vegetables before eating them. Traveler's diarrhea, caused by consuming contaminated water, unpasteurized milk and milk products, and unrefrigerated food, isn't a big problem—unless it happens to you. So watch what you eat, especially at outdoor buffets in the hot sun. Make sure cooked food is hot and cold food has been properly refrigerated.

The major health risk is sunburn or sunstroke. A long-sleeve shirt, a hat, and long pants or a beach wrap are essential on a boat, for midday at the beach, and whenever you go out sightseeing. Use sunscreen with an SPF of at least 15—especially if you're fair—and apply it liberally on your nose, ears, and other sensitive and exposed areas. Make sure the sunscreen is waterproof if you're engaging in water sports. Always limit your sun time for the first few days and drink plenty of liquids. Limit intake of caffeine and alcohol, which hasten dehydration.

Mosquitoes and flies can be bothersome, so pack strong repellent (the ones that contain DEET or Picaridin are the most effective). The strong trade winds are a relief in the subtropical climate, but don't hang your bathing suit on a balcony—it'll probably blow away. Help Arubans conserve water and energy: turn off air-conditioning when you leave your room, and don't let water run unattended.

Don't fly within 24 hours of scuba diving. In an emergency, Air Ambulance, run by Richard Rupert, will fly you to Curaçao at a low altitude if you need to get to a decompression chamber.

OVER-THE-COUNTER REMEDIES
There are a number of pharmacies and stores selling simple medications throughout the island (including at most hotels), and virtually anything obtainable in North America is available in Aruba.

SHOTS AND MEDICATIONS
No special vaccinations are required to visit Aruba.

Health Warnings National Centers for Disease Control & Prevention (*CDC*). ☎ *877/394–8747 international travelers' health line* ⊕ *www.cdc.gov/travel*. **World Health Organization** (*WHO*). ⊕ *www.who.int*.

┃ HOURS OF OPERATION

Bank hours are weekdays 8:15 to 5:45, with some branches closing for lunch from noon to 1. The Caribbean Mercantile Bank at the airport is open Saturday 9 to 4 and Sunday 9 to 1. The central post office in Oranjestad, catercorner to the San Francisco Church, is open weekdays 7:30 to noon and 1 to 4:30. Shops are generally open Monday through Saturday 8:30 to 6. Some stores close for lunch from noon to 2. Many shops also open when cruise ships are in port on Sunday and holidays.

HOLIDAYS

Aruba's official holidays are New Year's Day, Good Friday, Easter Sunday, and Christmas, as well as Betico Croes Day (January 25), National Anthem and Flag Day (March 18), Queen's Day (April 30), Labor Day (May 1), and Ascension Day (May 29 in 2014, May 14 in 2015).

▮ MAIL

From Aruba to the United States or Canada a letter costs Afl2.20 (about $1.25) and a postcard costs Afl1.30 (75¢). Expect it to take one to two weeks. When addressing letters to Aruba, don't worry about the lack of formal addresses or postal codes; the island's postal service knows where to go.

If you need to send a package in a hurry, there are a few options. The Federal Express office across from the airport offers overnight service to the United States if you get your package in before 3 pm. Another big courier service is UPS, and there are also several smaller local courier services that provide international deliveries, most of them open weekdays 9 to 5. Check the local phone book for details.

SHIPPING PACKAGES

Federal Express service is available in downtown Oranjestad.

Contacts FedEx ⊠ *Browninvest Financial Center, Wayaca 31A, Oranjestad* ☎ *297/592-9039.* **UPS** ⊠ *Rockefellerstraat 3, Oranjestad* ☎ *297/582-8646.*

▮ MONEY

Arubans happily accept U.S. dollars virtually everywhere. That said, there's no real need to exchange money, except for necessary pocket change (for soda machines or pay phones). The official currency is the Aruban florin (Afl), also called the guilder, which is made up of 100 cents. Silver coins come in denominations of 1, 2½, 5, 10, 25, and 50 (the square one) cents. Paper currency comes in denominations of 5, 10, 25, 50, and 100 florins.

Prices quoted throughout this book are in U.S. dollars unless otherwise noted.

Prices throughout this guide are given for adults. Substantially reduced fees are almost always available for children, students, and senior citizens.

ATMS AND BANKS

If you need fast cash, you'll find ATMs that accept international cards (and dispense cash in both U.S. and local currency) at banks in Oranjestad, at the major malls, and along the roads leading to the hotel strip.

Banks Caribbean Mercantile Bank ⊠ *Caya G.F. Betico Croes 5, Oranjestad* ☎ *297/582-3118.* **RBTT Bank** ⊠ *Caya G.F. Betico Croes 89, Oranjestad* ☎ *297/582-1515* ⊕ *www.rbtt.com.*

CREDIT CARDS

It's a good idea to inform your credit-card company before you travel, especially if you're going abroad and don't travel internationally very often. Otherwise, the credit-card company might put a hold on your card owing to unusual activity—not a good thing halfway through your trip. Record all your credit-card numbers—as well as the phone numbers to call if your cards are lost or stolen— in a safe place, so you're prepared should something go wrong. Both MasterCard and Visa have general numbers you can call (collect if you're abroad) if your card is lost, but you're better off calling the number of your issuing bank, since MasterCard and Visa usually just transfer you to your bank; your bank's number is usually printed on your card.

If you plan to use your credit card for cash advances, you'll need to apply for a PIN at least two weeks before your trip. Although it's usually cheaper (and safer) to use a credit card abroad for large purchases (so you can cancel payments or be reimbursed if there's a problem), note that some credit-card companies *and* the banks that issue them add substantial percentages to all foreign transactions, whether they're in a foreign currency or not. Check on these fees before leaving home, so there won't be any surprises when you get the bill.

Reporting Lost Cards American Express ☎ *800/528–4800 in U.S., 336/393–1111 collect from abroad* ⊕ *www.americanexpress.com.* **MasterCard** ☎ *800/627–8372 in U.S., 636/722–7111 collect from abroad* ⊕ *www.mastercard.com.* **Visa** ☎ *800/847–2911 in U.S., 410/581–9994 collect from abroad* ⊕ *www.visa.com.*

CURRENCY EXCHANGE
At this writing exchange rates were Afl1.79 to the U.S. dollar and Afl1.76 to the Canadian dollar. Stores, hotels, and restaurants converted at Afl1.80; supermarkets and gas stations at Afl1.75. The Dutch Antillean florin—used on Bonaire and Curaçao—isn't accepted here. Since U.S. dollars are universally accepted, few people exchange money.

Currency Conversion
Google ⊕ *www.google.com.* **Oanda.com** ⊕ *www.oanda.com.* **XE.com** ⊕ *www.xe.com.*

❚ PACKING

Dress on Aruba is generally casual. Bring loose-fitting clothing made of natural fabrics to see you through days of heat and humidity. Pack a beach cover-up, both to protect yourself from the sun and to provide something to wear to and from your hotel room. Bathing suits and immodest attire are frowned upon away from the beach. A sun hat is advisable, but you don't have to pack one—inexpensive straw hats are available everywhere. For shopping and sightseeing, bring walking shorts, jeans, T-shirts, long-sleeve cotton shirts, slacks, and sundresses. Nighttime dress can range from very informal to casually elegant, depending on the establishment. A tie is practically never required, but a jacket may be appropriate in fancy restaurants. You may need a light sweater or jacket for evening.

▮ PASSPORTS AND VISAS

A valid passport is required to enter or reenter the United States from Aruba.

▮ RESTROOMS

Outside Oranjestad, the only public restrooms you'll find will be in the few restaurants that dot the countryside.

Find a Loo The Bathroom Diaries. Flush with unsanitized info, the Bathroom Diaries locates, reviews, and rates restrooms the world over. ⊕ *www.thebathroomdiaries.com.*

▮ SAFETY

Arubans are very friendly, so you needn't be afraid to stop and ask anyone for directions. It's a relatively safe island, but commonsense rules still apply. Lock your rental car when you leave it, and leave valuables in your hotel safe. Don't leave bags unattended in the airport, on the beach, or on tour vehicles.

▮TIP➔ Distribute your cash, credit cards, IDs, and other valuables between a deep front pocket, an inside jacket or vest pocket, and a hidden money pouch. Don't reach for the money pouch once you're in public.

Contact Transportation Security Administration (*TSA*). ⊕ *www.tsa. gov.*

▮ TAXES

The airport departure tax is $37 for flights to the United States and $33.50 to other destinations, but the fee is usually included in your ticket price. Children under two don't pay departure tax. For purchases you'll pay a 3% BBO tax (a turnover tax on each level of sale for all goods and services) in all but the duty-free shops.

▮ TIME

Aruba is in the Atlantic standard time zone, which is one hour later than eastern standard time or four hours earlier than Greenwich mean time. During daylight saving time, between April and October, Atlantic standard is the same time as eastern daylight time.

Time Zones Timeanddate.com ⊕ *www.timeanddate.com/worldclock.*

▮ TIPPING

Restaurants generally include a 10%–15% service charge on the bill; when in doubt, ask. If service isn't included, a 15% tip is standard; if it's included, it's still customary to add something extra, usually small change, at your discretion. Taxi drivers expect a 10%–15% tip, but it isn't mandatory. Porters and bellhops should receive about $2 per bag; chambermaids about $2 a day, but check to see if their tips are included in your bill so you don't overpay.

▮ TOURS

You can see the main sights in one day, but set aside two days to really meander. Guided tours are your best option if you have only a short time.

TOUR OPERATORS

De Palm Tours has a near monopoly on Aruban sightseeing; you can make reservations through its general office or at hotel tour-desk branches. The company's basic 4½-hour tour hits the highlights. Wear tennis or hiking shoes, and bring a lightweight jacket or wrap (the air-conditioned bus gets cold). It begins at 9:30 am, picks you up in your hotel lobby, and costs $89 per person. A full-day Jeep Adventure tour ($107 per person) takes you to sights that would be difficult for you to find on your own and includes a stop at De Palm Island for a little fun in the water. Bring a bandanna to cover your mouth; the ride on rocky dirt roads can get dusty. Prices include round-trip airfare, transfers, sightseeing, and lunch; there's free time for shopping.

Romantic horse-drawn-carriage rides through the city streets of Oranjestad run $40 for a 30-minute tour; hours of operation are 7 pm to 11 pm, and carriages depart from the clock tower at the Royal Plaza Mall.

Contacts Aruba's Transfer Tour & Taxi ✉ *Pos Abao 41, Oranjestad* ☎ *297/582–2116.* **De Palm Tours** ✉ *L.G. Smith Blvd. 142, Oranjestad* ☎ *297/582–4400, 800/766–6016* ⊕ *www.depalm.com.*

SPECIAL-INTEREST TOURS

BOATING

If you try a cruise around the island, know that the choppy waters are stirred up by trade winds and that catamarans are much smoother than single-hulled boats. Sucking on a peppermint or lemon candy may help a queasy stomach; avoid boating with an empty or overly full stomach. Moonlight cruises cost about $40 per person. There are also snorkeling, dinner and dancing, and sunset party cruises to choose from, priced from $40 to $70 per person. Many of the smaller operators work out of their homes; they often offer to pick you up (and drop you off) at your hotel or meet you at a particular hotel pier.

Contacts De Palm Tours ✉ *L.G. Smith Blvd. 142, Oranjestad* ☎ *297/582–4400, 800/766–6016* ⊕ *www.depalm.com.* **Pelican Tours & Watersports** ✉ *J.E. Irausquin Blvd. 232, Oranjestad* ☎ *297/587–2302* ⊕ *www.pelican-aruba.com.* **Red Sail Sports** ✉ *Renaissance Mall, L.G. Smith Blvd. 82, Oranjestad* ☎ *297/586–1603, 877/733–7245 in U.S.* ⊕ *www.aruba-redsail.com.* **Seaworld Explorer** ☎ *297/582–4400* ⊕ *www.depalmtours.com/seaworld-explorer-semi-submarine.*

SUBMARINE TOURS

You can explore an underwater reef teeming with marine life without getting wet. Atlantis Submarines operates a 65-foot air-conditioned sub that takes 48 passengers 95 to 150 feet below the surface along Barcadera Reef. The two-hour trip (including boat transfer to the submarine platform and 50-minute plunge) costs $109. Make reservations one day in advance. Another option is the *Seaworld Explorer,* a semisubmersible also operated by Atlantis Submarines that allows you to view Aruba's marine habitat from

6 feet below the surface. The cost is $46 for a 1½-hour tour.

Contacts Atlantis Submarines ✉ *Renaissance Marina* ☎ *297/582–4400* ⊕ *www.depalmtours.com/atlantis-submarines-expedition.*

▌ TRIP INSURANCE

Comprehensive travel policies typically cover trip cancellation and interruption, letting you cancel or cut your trip short because of a personal emergency, illness, or, in some cases, acts of terrorism in your destination. Such policies also cover evacuation and medical care. Some also cover you for trip delays because of bad weather or mechanical problems as well as for lost or delayed baggage. Another type of coverage to look for is financial default—that is, when your trip is disrupted because a tour operator, airline, or cruise line goes out of business. Generally you must buy this when you book your trip or shortly thereafter, and it's only available to you if your operator isn't on a list of excluded companies.

At the very least, consider buying medical-only coverage. Neither Medicare nor some private insurers cover medical expenses anywhere outside the United States (including time aboard a cruise ship, even if it leaves from a U.S. port). Medical-only policies typically reimburse you for medical care (excluding that related to preexisting conditions) and hospitalization abroad, and provide for evacuation. You still have to pay the bills and await reimbursement from the insurer, though.

Another option is to sign up with a medical-evacuation assistance company. A membership in one of these companies gets you doctor referrals, emergency evacuation or repatriation, 24-hour hotlines for medical consultation, and other assistance. International SOS Assistance Emergency and AirMed International provide evacuation services and medical referrals. MedjetAssist offers medical evacuation.

Expect comprehensive travel insurance policies to cost about 4% to 8% of the total price of your trip (it's more like 8%–12% if you're over age 70). A medical-only policy may or may not be cheaper than a comprehensive policy. Always read the fine print of your policy to make sure that you're covered for the risks that are of most concern to you. Compare several policies to make sure you're getting the best price and range of coverage available.

▉TIP→ OK. You know you can save a bundle on trips to warm-weather destinations by traveling in rainy season. But there's also a chance that a severe storm will disrupt your plans. The solution? Look for hotels and resorts that offer storm/hurricane guarantees. Although they rarely allow refunds, most guarantees do let you rebook later if a storm strikes.

Comprehensive Travel Insurers Access America ☎ *866/729–6021* ⊕ *www.accessamerica.com.* **AIG Travel Guard** ☎ *800/826–4919* ⊕ *www.travelguard.com.* **CSA Travel Protection** ☎ *800/873–9855* ⊕ *www.csatravelprotection.com.*

HTH Worldwide ☎ *610/254-8700* ⊕ *www.hthworldwide.com.* **Travelex Insurance** ☎ *888/228-9792* ⊕ *www. travelex-insurance.com.* **Travel Insured International** ☎ *800/243-3174* ⊕ *www.travelinsured.com.*

Insurance Comparison Sites **Insure My Trip.com** ☎ *800/487-4722* ⊕ *www.insuremytrip.com.* **Square Mouth.com** ☎ *800/240-0369, 727/490-5803* ⊕ *www.squaremouth.com.*

Medical Assistance Companies **AirMed International Medical Group** ⊕ *www.airmed.com).* **International SOS** ⊕ *www.internationalsos.com.* **MedjetAssist** ⊕ *www.medjetassist.com.*

Medical-Only Insurers **International Medical Group** ☎ *800/628-4664* ⊕ *www.imglobal.com.* **Wallach & Company** ☎ *800/237-6615, 540/687-3166* ⊕ *www.wallach.com.*

❙ VISITOR INFORMATION

Before leaving home, contact the Aruba Tourism Authority at one of its many offices. On Aruba the tourist office has free brochures and information officers who are ready to answer any questions you may have, weekdays 7:30 am–4:30 pm.

The Caribbean Tourism Organization (⊕ *www.onecaribbean. org*), which has information on the island, is another good resource.

Aruba Information **Aruba Tourism Authority** ✉ *L.G. Smith Blvd. 172, Eagle Beach* ☎ *954/767-6477 in Fort Lauderdale, 201/330-0800 in Weehawken, NJ, 297/582-3777 in Aruba* ⊕ *www.aruba.com.*

❙ WEDDINGS

People over the age of 18 can marry as long as they submit the appropriate documents 14 days in advance. Couples are required to submit birth certificates with raised seals, through the mail or in person, to Aruba's Office of the Civil Registry. They also need an apostil—a document proving they're free to marry—from their country of residence.

With so many beautiful spots to choose from, weddings on Aruba are guaranteed to be romantic. And be sure to register for the island's "One Cool Honeymoon" program for special discounts from local businesses. Ask your hotel for more information.

Aruba Weddings for You. This small company's services include securing a location on the island, submitting legal documents, confirming arrangements with suppliers, decorating the venue, and coordinating the ceremony. ⊕ *www.arubaweddingsforyou.com.*

Information **Aruba Fairy Tales** ☎ *297/993-0045* 🖶 *297/583-1511* ⊕ *www.arubafairytales.com.* **Aruba Weddings for You.** This small company's services include securing a location on the island, submitting legal documents, confirming arrangements with suppliers, decorating the venue, and coordinating the ceremony. ✉ *Nune 92, Paradera* ☎ *297/583-7638* 🖶 *297/588-6073* ⊕ *www.arubaweddingsforyou.com.*

Arubus ⊕ *www.arubus.com.*

INDEX

PHOTO CREDITS

Fodor's InFocus ARUBA

Publisher: Amanda D'Acierno, *Senior Vice President*

Editorial: Arabella Bowen, *Executive Editorial Director*; Linda Cabasin, *Editorial Director*

Design: Fabrizio La Rocca, *Vice President, Creative Director*; Tina Malaney, *Associate Art Director*; Chie Ushio, *Senior Designer*; Ann McBride, *Production Designer*

Photography: Melanie Marin, *Associate Director of Photography*; Jessica Parkhill and Jennifer Romains, *Researchers*

Maps: Rebecca Baer, *Senior Map Editor*; David Lindroth, Ed Jacobus, William Wu, with additional cartography provided by Henry Colomb, Mark Stroud, and Ali Baird, Moon Street Cartography, *Cartographers*

Production: Linda Schmidt, *Managing Editor*; Evangelos Vasilakis, *Associate Managing Editor*; Angela L. McLean, *Senior Production Manager*

Sales: Jacqueline Lebow, *Sales Director*

Marketing & Publicity: Heather Dalton, *Marketing Director*; Katherine Fleming, *Senior Publicist*

Business & Operations: Susan Livingston, *Vice-President, Strategic Business Planning*; Sue Daulton, *Vice-President, Operations*

Fodors.com: Megan Bell, *Executive Director, Revenue & Business Development*; Yasmin Marinaro, *Senior Director, Marketing & Partnerships*

Series Editor: Douglas Stallings

Editor: Eric B. Wechter

Writer: Vernon O'Reilly-Ramesar

Production Editor: Evangelos Vasilakis

4th Edition

ISBN 978-0-8041-4168-0

ISSN 1939-988X

SPECIAL SALES

This book is available at special discounts for bulk purchases for sales promotions or premiums. For more information, e-mail specialmarkets@randomhouse.com

PRINTED IN CHINA

10 9 8 7 6 5 4 3 2 1

ABOUT OUR WRITER

Vernon O'Reilly-Ramesar is the Head of Current Affairs and a television broadcaster for ieTV in Trinidad, and divides his time between Toronto and the southern Caribbean. Currently based in Trinidad and Tobago, Vernon tours the region extensively for both work and pleasure. In his spare time he enjoys exploring the miracles of Trinidad's rain forests and absorbing the complex local cultures. Over the years he has forged friendships on all the islands he visits. Vernon has contributed to Fodor's guides, including Fodor's *Caribbean,* for more than 10 years. The author would like to thank the Aruba Tourism Authority for their help in gathering information for this book.